A STAR'S PASSIONATE LOVE AFFAIRS

WARREN BEATTY— In public, they were beautiful to behold. In private, there were screaming fights and slammed doors.

ELVIS PRESLEY—She hooked him when every girl in America wanted him. But while he hid from his fans, she had to hide from his jealous mama.

STEVE McQUEEN—Sexy outlaws on a motorcycle, their scenes were steamy both in front of and behind the camera.

A STAR'S SHOCKING SECRETS

Her wild mood swings, paralyzing fears, pills, liquor, and the depressions that led to a hushed-up suicide attempt years before her controversial and tragic death.

AS ONLY A STAR'S SISTER CAN REVEAL THEM!

They talked about everything—when they were talking—sharing notes and, sometimes, lovers. Beautiful, exciting, sophisticated sisters—produced and created in Hollywood.

NATALIE

LANA WOOD

A DELL BOOK

Published by
Dell Publishing Co., Inc.
1 Dag Hammarskjold Plaza
New York, New York 10017

ISBN: 0-440-16268-8

Reprinted by arrangement with G. P. Putnam's Sons
Printed in the United States of America
First Dell printing—June 1985

To
Natalie
Right or Wrong
Good or Bad
You are Special
and
Pop
Misunderstood
But Greatly Loved . . .

1

She stood before two big cars, occasionally wringing her hands in anticipation, nervously shuffling her feet in the sand. There were many lights, but there were many shadows as well, forming sharp contrasts in the dark night. Most of the lights were on her and the two cars, a few others on the crowd of young extras gathered to the side.

She was wearing a white blouse with a pretty collar, a full blue skirt, and she was also wearing a great deal of makeup, especially around her eyes and on her lips. As always, she wore a bracelet on her left wrist. Her clothes, her face, and her beauty were the look of her time and to me she was the most incredibly beautiful young woman I had ever seen. I saw her every day and she was always beautiful, but just now, standing on the edge of a steep palisade, the ocean pounding at the beach below, the lights scattering their glare about the edge of the cliff, she seemed almost beyond belief.

The expression on her face was serious and she was obviously frightened and excited. She kept look-

ing to the stunt coordinator, to the director, and then
to James Dean, who was sitting in one of the cars.
Whenever she looked at him, she would smile. From
time to time she also turned and looked to where our
mother and I stood, and for us the smile was reassuring. Every time she smiled at us I would feel better,
but the feeling never lasted. The tension—hers, the
director's, the other actors', and the crew's—was almost palpable. My mother's hand held mine and I
felt her grip tighten every time she heard somebody
shout an order.

Finally the director gave his order. Natalie quickly
walked off to the side of the cars away from us, and
when he signaled her with a quick move of his hand,
she ran back to the area just ahead of and between
the two big cars. She threw her arms up into the air,
shouted, "Hit your lights!" and brought her arms
flying down to her sides just as she jumped into the
air. The cars roared toward her, and I buried my face
in my mother's skirts, terrified and in tears. Natalie
was in danger, or at least that is how I perceived it. I
was eight, and the differences between making movies and reality were not exactly clear to me. Movies
were a constant in our lives; they determined what we
did every waking moment. They were not to be questioned.

Terror is my greatest memory of this scene from
Rebel Without a Cause, and I remember too that for
some hours after the scene was shot—there were
several takes, and each time, I turned away and hid

my face—I kept asking my mother if Natalie was all right.

"Of course, of course," she would tell me, but I was not easily convinced and it was not until Natalie was back in her dressing room, sitting before her mirror while her makeup was being removed, and I was sitting cross-legged on the floor, that I began to believe all was well again. It was late now, and I was so relieved that I began to fall asleep, sitting there listening to Natalie, watching her. Even without the makeup, the clothing, and all the other trappings of her profession, she was beautiful. I wanted to be just like her, and I knew in my heart—and in my mirror—that the prospect was more than hopeless; it was simply impossible.

I was skinny and my legs were like toothpicks with knots in them because my knees were always skinned. I was shy, I had few friends, and I spent nearly all of my time reading or playing with the pets we had at home, including the mouse I kept in a shoebox under my bed. Natalie knew about the mouse—we shared many secrets—but my mother did not and I lived in fear she would find out. It wasn't likely, though, because my mother didn't have much interest in house-keeping and seldom bothered to look under our beds or in our closets. Besides, I knew if my mouse was discovered, I could count on Natalie to come to my rescue.

Natalie was sixteen, gregarious, with big dark eyes and thick dark hair. Boys flowed in and out of our house, and every arrival and departure—plus all that went on in between—was carefully monitored by Mother. Natalie, after all, was a star. Not only that, she had done the impossible: she had begun as a child star, then moved gracefully through adolescence, and had remained a star. She remained one until her death.

I was expected to follow in her footsteps. I was supposed to work, become an actress, and hit stardom like Natalie. At the time I took it as a way of life, a given. For some time I thought movies were what everybody did, but now I was no longer certain. I knew for sure that they were what my family did. My father worked in the studios and my mother was lady-in-waiting to Natalie the star—and I tagged along too when Natalie made films. School was attended when movies didn't interfere; we went to class at the studio. We were both good students, and if I had one claim to superiority over Natalie, it was school. I was smart, quick, and my grades—with the exception of gym, which I wasn't taught in studio schools and which I failed regularly in public schools—were straight A.

Studying was easy; attending school wasn't. I always sat at the back of the class, usually alone, and dreaded being called on to answer questions. One day at the studio school, my pencil broke and I could not summon up the courage to ask the teacher for permission to sharpen it. I sat there trying to memorize the questions I was supposed to be writing down. The teacher finally noticed that I was not writing, and asked me why. My answer was a whisper and she had to ask me two more times what the problem was before she heard me. All the other students burst into laughter. I burst into tears, fled the room, and would not go back the next day. I read by myself instead, did all my lessons on my own, and turned them in when I finally went back to class.

My problem—and Natalie's too, though she had begun to outgrow it by now—was that while we were good at school, we felt we were good at something that was essentially unimportant. Our mother was unimpressed by scholarship. She felt that girls did not need an education. They needed stardom or good marriages, preferably both. It was Natalie who encouraged my academic aspirations, and that was all I needed. When I asked to be put in a full-time public school like other children, my mother could not understand why. Natalie did, and it was because of Natalie that I was finally taken out of the studio school and sent to public school. But not for long. My acting career, which had up to now been a series of brief starts and sudden stops necessitated by Natalie's busy schedule, would soon begin in earnest.

When *Rebel* was finished and screened, at last I could watch the car race without fearing for Natalie's life. I sat engrossed as I relived the moment and then saw the cars go careening off the cliff, James Dean the victor in the chicken contest. It would go on to become one of the classic films of the 1950's, and it did much to secure Natalie's place at the top of the list of the most popular stars in the world. She remained friends with Nicholas Ray, the director, and for many years she was close to her co-stars Nick Adams and Sal Mineo. She also had a brief and intense friendship with Jimmy Dean, who spent most of his time away from the filming with her. Nick, Sal, and Jimmy were often at our home, sitting out around the pool, eating, laughing, and playing games. I remember once discovering that if you turned a flashlight off and on fast enough and performed in pantomine, it gave the illusion of a silent movie. One of my friends and I put on a show, and everybody left the pool to come and watch us; Jimmy and Sal, Nick and Natalie were all kind, tolerant, and encouraging to me—enthusiastic supporters of my small attempts to shed my shyness. Natalie went especially out of her way to strengthen her little sister with intelligent and effective nurturing.

One by one Jimmy and Nick and Sal died—early and tragically—and finally Natalie joined them. I cannot look at *Rebel,* cannot look at any of Natalie's films now. When I see them on television, I turn the set off. If my daughter is watching the film, I leave the room. My mother, on the other hand, lives in a world filled with Natalie, her movies, her scrapbooks, her memories. When she is not living in the present of my own life, she is living in Natalie's past. She sees Natalie's children; I do not. She sees Robert Wagner, Natalie's last husband, from time to time; I do not. I have asked her many times why it is I am not allowed to see my nieces, why my former brother-in-law does not return my phone calls or answer my letters, yet my own daughter is taken by her grandmother to see her cousins (but only when I am at work and not aware the visit is about to take place). Her only answer is that I should call R.J., Wagner's nickname, and apologize. She does not know what I am to apologize for, and neither do I. When I say I have called and that he does not return my calls, she says nothing.

2

Natalie Wood's breakthrough in films occurred when she was five, and if it sounds like a Hollywood fantasy, that's because it was. She was Natasha Gurdin, the daughter of a housewife and a laborer—Russian immigrants who barely spoke English—and the Gurdin family was just getting by, living on the edge of poverty in Santa Rosa, California, a small town near San Francisco. Our few family pictures show her to be a tiny, pretty girl with luminous dark eyes, eyes a writer would later call "as large and as shining as a November moon."

Natasha as a child was mischievous, energetic, a chatterbox, given to pranks which sometimes got her into trouble. My mother remembers walking down the streets of Santa Rosa with Natasha at her side; others as they approached would nod in greeting—it was the custom in those days in small towns to be friendly to strangers—and just as they nodded, their friendly greetings would turn to a look of fury. My mother insists she did not understand what was happening until one day she looked down and caught

Natasha crossing her eyes, sticking out her tongue, and giving the passing ladies' dresses a quick hoist.

All of Santa Rosa was agog about *Happy Land;* Don Ameche and Frances Dee had come to shoot in our town and they were being directed by a man named Irving Pichel. One day Mr. Pichel put out a call for extras, and one of the first to show up was Marie Gurdin with her daughter Natasha. Her other daughter, Olga, was thirteen and at school. Natasha had been instructed to curtsy when she met the director and to look directly at him and to smile. She did exactly as she was told and Mr. Pichel decided Natasha would do just fine. With one condition: she was to take a bite out of an ice-cream cone, drop it, and burst into tears. Could she cry on cue?

"Of course she can," our mother replied. And of course Natasha did.

Months went by and one day the telephone rang. It was Mr. Pichel, asking if Natalie could come to Hollywood to make a screen test for his new film, *Tomorrow Is Forever.*

"Of course she can," Mother replied. Mother had left Russia as a child; she had left China as a young woman with a small child; picking up and leaving Santa Rosa was a piece of cake. With only the promise of a screen test, Mother packed everybody up and —with her husband's silent agreement—moved the entire family to Hollywood.

Natasha flunked her screen test. Years later she used to say it was because of the big upheaval in her life, the move, the anxiety, Mother's fierce determi-

nation. Whatever it was, Natalie's tears did not flow
on cue this time.

Crisis. Little money, a new and strange city, a cal-
culated risk gone completely wrong. That didn't stop
Mother. She marched over to Twentieth Century-
Fox and talked herself into Mr. Pichel's inner sanc-
tum. I don't think she got in because of being especially persuasive. She probably got in because she
purposely fractured her English so that people kept
passing her through gates and receptionists because
they couldn't understand her. Once she was in Mr.
Pichel's office, her English improved remarkably,
and her ability to charm and cajole soared. She
emerged with Mr. Pichel's promise that Natasha
could have another screen test.

Natasha, of course, was terrified. It was Olga—who
had been studying drama at San Jose High School
and who would have loved to be in Natasha's place—
who figured out how to get Natasha to cry. She reminded Natasha of the day a few years before when
the two of them were standing at a gas station having
a bottle of soda pop. Their dog spotted them from
across the street and came running. A car hit him as
he crossed the street and killed him. At the time Olga
had pulled Natasha away from the scene and instructed her not to look. Natasha looked anyway and
began weeping. For the screen test, Olga instructed
her little sister to close her eyes for a moment and
relive that experience.

Natasha got the part. Her co-stars were Claudette
Colbert, Orson Welles, and George Brent. Mr. Pichel

felt that "Natasha Gurdin" was not quite the right name, and so "Natasha" translated into "Natalie" and "Gurdin" was changed to "Wood," after Mr. Pichel's friend the director Sam Wood. Natalie not only cried on cue, she all but stole the film.

She was a natural, Mr. Pichel announced, one of those rare creatures the camera loved. He had several sons, and Natalie became like a daughter to him. He asked Mother if he could legally adopt Natalie, and while Mother would not hear of it, she managed to issue such a diplomatic refusal that Mr. Pichel remained her and Natalie's friend for the rest of his life. It was he who helped subdue Mother's fierce ambition a bit, so that life for Natalie would at least be halfway normal.

Natalie made her next film, *The Bride Wore Boots*, the same year, 1945, and again Mr. Pichel was her director. When the picture came out a year later, there was no doubt about it: Natalie was a star and she was going to be around for a while.

From then on she was a commodity whose life was controlled by two forces, her mother and her studio. My mother never left her side, and there was a social worker on hand as well—a legal requirement which my mother managed to accept politely just as long as the social worker wasn't too assertive about matters such as schoolwork. Natalie was allowed no friends of her own, no one to gossip with, and certainly no boys were permitted around her. She was expected to curtsy before all adults, which she did until she was fifteen and rebelled. It was a significant moment. But for now there was no rebellion, just a dutiful child doing exactly as she was told. Mother also managed to get Pop a job in the studio, first as a carpenter and then—he was a naturally talented artist—in the special-effects department. She took care of every detail, even to making sure Natalie could keep all the clothes she wore in her films. Only one thing took my mother away from Natalie's side. Me.

On March 1, 1946, my mother surmounted her terror of hospitals for the third time in her life and had her third daughter. They named me Svetlana, but began immediately to call me Lana. My father was in New York with Natalie when I was born, and the person who carried me in and presented me to my mother was my eighteen-year-old sister. Life was becoming increasingly difficult for Olga, and my arrival only complicated matters. We have talked about it for years, Olga and I, and we remain close friends despite the great differences in our lives. Olga is my half-sister, born in China when my mother was married to her first husband. He eventually immigrated to the United States, and when my mother was able to follow two years later, she arrived to find him living with another woman. End of marriage.

Olga felt increasingly out of place in our family. Mother's entire energies were focused exclusively on Natalie, and now there was me. To make matters worse, the rumor that I was actually Olga's illegitimate child began to make the rounds of her high school. Olga had her own dreams, her own life to lead. She was old enough to understand that she was destined to become a satellite. She felt, she later told me, an outcast. When Natalie was given ballet lessons, Olga asked to have them too. She was refused; the reason given was that we did not have the money. Natalie's money, by court order, was put away, and we lived on my father's income. Olga was miserable.

Within the first year of my life, Olga left home and went back to northern California to live with her father. It was a wise decision. She was welcomed into his family and remained with him until she married. She has three sons, all of whom are successes in their professions, and she is now happily smothered with grandchildren.

Natalie made *The Miracle on Thirty-fourth Street* the year I was born, a film which went on to become what we would jokingly refer to as "Natalie's first classic." The film is a Christmas-holiday perennial on TV to this day, and for many years I watched it. Never again.

The first years of my life, I was bundled off to the studio along with Mother and Natalie. Whenever they went out at night to a premiere or some other event requiring Natalie's presence, I was left at home with my father. Natalie's evenings out were strictly chaperoned. She was almost always at home and in bed by ten in order to be refreshed and ready to work the next morning.

While Natalie filmed *Driftwood*, I made my movie debut. I played what was intended to be an adorable little baby, one of those who elicit oohs and ahs from audiences. Instead, I cried. My part ended up on the cutting-room floor. Mother, meanwhile, had become friendly with Merle Oberon, and one day while Natalie was in studio school Mother took me to the stage to show me off to the legendary star of *Wuthering Heights*. I am told—several thousand times by now—that I was scooped up by Miss Oberon and place in her lap. Miss Oberon was in costume and in between scenes when she cuddled me on her lap. I did what any other little baby would do, and it was some time before Miss Oberon's costume was dried and the stain removed. Years later I met her at a dinner party and she had no recollection of the event, perhaps because she asked me, "Which picture was I on?" and I could not answer. Some actresses have a special frame of reference.

Driftwood is memorable for one incident, one that was not intended and almost ended Natalie's career. At one point in the film she was to walk across a wooden bridge, and just as she reached the other side, the bridge was to collapse. The stunt was rehearsed and carefully planned, but when it was finally shot, a cue somewhere was misunderstood and the bridge collapsed when Natalie was in the middle of it, sending her plummeting a good ten feet onto the floor of the stage.

When the debris was cleared and the doctors had done their work—all at the studio because mother hates hospitals—Natalie was bruised and shaken but not seriously injured. The bone in her left wrist was distended, and the doctors recommended surgery. Mother refused, and because at the time Natalie shared her terror of hospitals and was equally terrified of disagreeing with Mother, she refused too. She wore bracelets to hide the deformed wrist for the rest of her life.

The rules for Natalie were strict and unwavering. She was taught from the beginning that at all times she was to be Natalie Wood. She learned her lessons well—Natalie was dutiful and determined—and so she became Natalie Wood. It was a transformation which would dominate all our lives. Even after her death she seemed to be somehow present, an indelible force which would be a part of our lives forever. It has diminished with time, but not much.

For me, there was a different set of rules. I was given much more freedom, little direction, and most of the time did whatever I wanted to do. This double standard did not seem at all unusual, at least not until some years later. I was in awe of my sister. An entourage surrounded her, attentive and solicitous. A smile or a caress from Natalie, or a talk with her— these were the highlights of my life. She had many smiles for me, and was always ready to talk, to answer all of my questions. Not even my own mother was that patient. Mother rarely touched me. We were not an affectionate family, and hugs and kisses were reserved for special occasions. Natalie and I were made to sleep with our hands outside the covers, and it was not until I was grown that I understood why. On cold nights in our house both of us would snuggle into bed, roll up into balls, and begin to fall asleep, only to have Mother come into the room. We both pre-

tended to be turning over, but what we were doing
was putting our hands outside the covers. Mother
must have been afraid we were sexually curious
babes, but we weren't.

Natalie was my surrogate parent, the person I
knew would protect me from any danger. One night
Mother got us up in matching red dresses and she
and Pop took us out to dinner. We were driving
across a bridge when Natalie saw a car strike a child.
Natalie gasped in horror, and when I looked up to
see what was happening, Natalie pulled me into her
lap and hid my face in her arms. I struggled a bit as
my curiosity got the best of me, but Natalie's embrace was as complete as it was tense, and I remained
in her arms, my face buried on her chest. She held me
hard, her body rigid. I knew I was safe.

She was always working. In 1949 and again in
1950, she starred in four pictures, making them back-
to-back, with seldom more than a weekend between
them. I was usually on the set when she filmed, confused about all those people she called Mother and
Father, people who changed from picture to picture.
I resented sharing her with all those mothers and
fathers, the mothers in particular, because she already had one mother who was so clearly in charge
and whose judgments were not to be questioned.

In 1952 she made *The Star* with Bette Davis and
Sterling Hayden. It was the beginning of a lifelong
friendship with Bette Davis, formed in one of Bette's
typical displays of strong character. Natalie was fourteen, midway through adolescence, and just begin-

ning to assert herself. One day it came time to shoot a scene which Natalie had spotted early on when she first read the script. She said then she could not do what the scene required and that they should get her a double. Natalie could not swim well and she was terrified of water. The scene took place on a boat and in it she was required to jump off the boat and swim in the ocean.

We were all on board the boat, bobbing in the water off the coast of Los Angeles. There was no double and Natalie was ordered to jump. She balked. She was told there was no other way to shoot the scene. Natalie was in tears, ready to take the plunge, when she reminded the director once again she had said from the very start that she couldn't do the scene. Miss Davis heard the commotion, arrived on deck, and listened to Natalie's protest. No other actress has fought for her rights with the same mixture of ferocity and integrity as Bette Davis, and all of this —and more, because a child was involved—was now brought to the fore. Natalie, she said, would not only not do the scene, but if any more orders to the contrary were attempted, Miss Davis would walk off the set and close down the picture.

Natalie's terror of swimming in the ocean provided her first understanding of power, its uses and its privileges. She always said that it was Bette Davis who first caused her to realize that speaking up—and out—wasn't a bad thing to do.

3

In 1953 Natalie made a film which was so bad it is a wonder several careers weren't totally ruined. The picture was *The Silver Chalice*, a Roman soap opera memorable for any number of awful moments. Paul Newman, be-togaed, his hair combed down across his forehead and curled Caesar-style, performed the whole picture without once turning red from embarrassment. Natalie, playing Virginia Mayo as a young woman, had to wear contact lenses and had her hair dyed blond. Nothing looks quite so dyed as a dark Russian beauty bleached beyond belief, and Natalie spent months with her hair under a scarf. She wore the contact lenses about two days before abandoning them, and if anyone noticed that her eyes changed colors near the start of her part, no one mentioned it.

The Silver Chalice turned up on prime-time television years later and Paul Newman took an ad in the Hollywood trade papers to formally apologize for the film and his performance, a gesture which was greeted with much laughter. He has a good sense of humor about what I've heard him call his turkeys.

Natalie took it all much more seriously, and when it came to career mistakes she had no sense of humor at all. It wasn't until many films and many years later that Natalie was heard to remark she should have shared the public apologia with her co-star.

By the time *The Silver Chalice* was made, we were all living in a sprawling ranch house in the San Fernando Valley, in Northridge. It was all country then, and we had a huge piece of land filled with walnut trees, wild growth, and all the pets we wanted. Mother, who had her own special sense of design, filled the large house, with its beamed ceilings and hardwood floors, with brightly colored, lacquered Chinese furniture.

Natalie worked long hours, and I spent most of my time at the studios or, if he was between jobs, at home with my father. I became very attached to him; I'd burst into tears if he got up in the morning and announced he was going to work. Mother was central to Natalie's life, and he was central to mine. Natalie was negotiating her way through the shoals of Mom's opposition—to call it vehement is to understate the case—to any form of dating. Natalie was a young woman, but not so grown up that she was opposed to hikes and games with me. On those days she was not working, we would be out early and play all day.

It was also the only time I remember my parents doing anything in the way of entertaining. They never had many friends, and those they did have did not usually last long. The combination of my mother's obsession with Natalie's career and my father's remoteness made the maintenance of friendships difficult if not impossible. English was the second language in our home then, and I have hardly any memory of its being spoken on social occasions because nearly all of our family's friends were Russian.

My participation in the Gurdin family social life was nil. I was shy, awkward, and withdrawn. Natalie, who was accustomed to being around adults all of the time, was self-assured and sociable. I was not. With the exception of my sister, I had no friends, no playmates except occasionally one of the other children in the neighborhood. But never for long, because every time I formed a relationship it would be interrupted while I spent a few weeks at the studio with Natalie and Mom. I thought such a situation the rule, not the exception. And I also saw nothing unusual in my habit, whenever we had company, of sitting on the floor of my closet, the door closed, happily playing with the elaborate dollhouse my father had built for me.

It had two stories, large elegant rooms, and lots of furniture. I would push my shoes and toys aside and make room for a large yard. That was where I did my entertaining. My dolls were perfectly dressed, always elegant, and each of them was an extension of me. I had parties and I had picnics, always with other families and their children. There were lots of children at my dollhouse parties, and lots of things for them to do. They also liked one another. There was no squabbling, no unhappiness, no feelings of fear or doubt. It was a microcosm of a perfect world, and when I was in it, I was happy.

Our menagerie of pets grew every time a stray turned up. We had fun playing with our hamsters, parakeets, cockatoos, and a horse. One day Natalie and I found a baby squirrel that had been abandoned by his mother, and we took him home and turned him into a house pet. He was charming and antic, but also decidedly sloppy in his personal habits and given to chewing on the corners of the piano legs. He also demolished Natalie's collection of the busts of famous composers, those small white statues made out of a rough substance which is more like salt than marble. We finally took him into the yard and put him in a tree, but invariably we found him crouching by the door, waiting to come in, whenever we returned home. Eventually he took up residence in the tree and was still there when we moved out. Natalie had a particular affinity for birds and horses. She kept a cockatoo in her bedroom and often it spent the night perched on the bedstead.

The animals Natalie had that weren't live were stuffed toys; they filled her room at all times. Later, when she began dating R.J., she went on a redecorating binge, with the result that her room was crammed with stuffed tigers—and R.J. started calling her Tiger. The tigers disappeared when Natalie fashioned her first grown-up bedroom, featuring an Early American canopy bed with a quilted chintz spread and pillow covers all in a dusty pink color. There were ruffles everywhere, and the furniture was all maple. When it was done she stood looking at it, scratching her chin in concentration.

"I think I overdid it," she finally announced. That's a fair description of Natalie's interior decorating. But, like anything she set out to learn, she ultimately mastered the art of design. It just took longer than most of her undertakings.

Her room, regardless of the decor of the moment, contained her drawings of her pets and of the things around our home she liked best. She was a natural artist, like our father, and it was her interest in art which eventually led her to collecting fine art. She would sit on her bed, her legs tucked under her, her sketchbook in her lap, her concentration complete. She encouraged me to draw, too, and while Natalie could produce a perfectly proportioned horse, the best I could do was a somewhat undernourished tree.

"That's nice, Lana. Now try a cat."

I scribbled away, my tongue screwed into my cheek, while Natalie, the picture of grace, sketched happily. When I was done I'd show her my latest effort. My cats looked exactly like my trees. Except to Natalie.

Our ranch house was on a good-sized piece of land and we had all the animals we wanted. At last we had a family life, and to Natalie and me it was idyllic. This was the way we had seen people live in the movies and we actually began to feel normal, with a few odd exceptions. One winter there were several storms, with thunder and lightning, and we endured them sleeping curled up on inflated rubber mattresses which Mother devoutly believed protected us from being struck by lightning.

Natalie's horse was a palomino named Powder, a horse she bought from the studio. He could paw the ground, count his age, bow, and do all sorts of tricks. He was also, on occasion and never predictably, high-strung. Natalie adored him, and so did I. We usually rode him together, and after a while Natalie would get off, take the reins in her hand, and walk awhile, letting me pretend I was riding him all by myself. One autumn day we spent the whole afternoon riding him around the neighborhood, and near the end of the ride Natalie dismounted and began leading Powder as I sat alone.

Some other children rode by on their bicycles, shooting off their cap guns and shouting. Powder spooked and sent me flying. When I finally hit the ground, he kicked me in the head with a rear leg. I was unconscious for a week, perhaps more, but I'd briefly come to. I have a vivid memory of Natalie sitting beside the bed, weeping, holding my hand, Mother hovering in the background. My mother refused to have me taken to a hospital, and instead turned Natalie's and my bedroom into a sick bay, complete with the necessary machines, twenty-four-hour nurses, and a doctor who came by each day.

When I finally came to it was Natalie who was sitting beside me, perched on the edge of her chair. She mopped my brow, and smiled, and I was disturbed to see there were tears streaming down her cheeks.

"Natalie, I'm so sorry."

"Shh. Everything is going to be all right now. You'll be fine." She took my hand, and I drifted off to sleep, sure it would be safe now because Natalie was right beside me.

I was mortified by the thought that I had caused so much trouble, had disrupted our family life and, most important, Natalie's career. I had multiple skull fractures and they would require time—and attention—to heal. Up until the accident I had made my way through life by being as inconspicuous and silent as I could be; now I'd ruined everything.

Guilt-stricken, Natalie sold the horse immediately. She never left my side, heaping love and reassurance on me. It wasn't long until I was well enough to enjoy all the attention she was giving me. Our mother would bustle about, chatting in Russian so that the nurse wouldn't hear her conversations, telling me I was getting much better, Natalie would soon be returning to the studios, it was all an accident. Natalie did not agree that it was an accident, and for some time afterward held herself responsible. Finally Mother decided a change of scene would improve everything, and so, without any discussion at all—Natalie and I still wanted to live in the house but were not consulted—she sold the place and bought a much smaller house on Valley Vista Boulevard in the foothills of Sherman Oaks.

The calamity with the horse came to be remembered differently by all of us. Several years went by before Natalie absolved herself of her feelings of guilt. I never for one minute held her responsible and said so whenever the subject came up. Olga, who was pregnant with her first child when it happened, remembers being angry that Mother did not break the news until my multiple fractures had begun to heal, and was informed it was a servant who was walking the horse, not Natalie. Mother still maintains that is how it happened. Whenever the subject arose and Mother would make her pronouncement, Natalie and I would shoot one another looks and Natalie would roll her eyes to the heavens. We never, ever had a servant.

If there had been a maid around, maybe there'd have been some order in the household. Our pets made a mess of the place, and Mother was as oblivious of the squalor as I was. For a woman who was engineering the career of one of the most famous young women in the world, she was oddly casual about clothing and cleanliness. Neither Natalie nor I was ever ordered to the bath after a day of play. Natalie, of course, had a makeup woman, a wardrobe woman, and all the other studio staff telling her what to do, setting an example for her. Natalie grew up squeaky clean and neat as a pin. Because of Natalie, I grew up that way too. To this day I associate a clean closet, a shower, or a shampoo with order and sense. And with Natalie. Within an hour after I learned of her death, with our entire world falling apart around us, paramedics in the living room taking care of my mother, I marched upstairs and shampooed my hair. Not since I was a child, and Natalie was the resident giver of shampoos, had I washed my hair in the sink. That day I did, and only when I was done could I begin to deal with chaos and devastation.

Natalie's clothing came directly from the studio and mine came from shopping trips with Mother. When I grew up enough to wear Natalie's clothing, she was always generous with it. Consequently, I spent my teens as a clothes horse, and I remain addicted to fashion. Times when the urge to go shopping overwhelms me are known to friends as the Lana-needs-to-mainline-clothing days. The size of the dose is determined by the size of the bank balance, though there have been times when the former completely wrecked the latter.

Natalie, too, loved clothes and shopping, loved to look ravishing. And she usually did. As adults our style of dressing diverged, Natalie preferring soft, feminine clothing and me the more tailored look. It took some years for our individual styles to emerge. By that time her world was more feminine and romantic. Mine was not. I am, as she once said, "more casual."

From her teens until the last time I saw her, Natalie was perfectly groomed and always made up. Always. Even when she was getting up in the morning with virtually nothing to do—a rare occurrence—she would go to her dressing table after her bath, sit down, and put on her makeup. By her forties the only time I saw her not completely made-up was the day we drove together to the dermatologist to get our faces peeled. Even then she wore eye liner and mascara, which she removed in the doctor's office. It wasn't, at least not at first, a sign of vanity. It was communicated to her that she must always be "on" as Natalie Wood, and that meant always looking like a movie star. She became a master of makeup and said to me, "In a pinch, I could always get work in pictures as a makeup artist."

Later, as her children began to grow and she was past forty, she looked to the makeup to hide those few signs of age she was beginning to show. She would even practice poses to hide her incipient double chin. She had a slightly chubby face and it bothered her. On more average-sized people a slight weight gain is indiscernible. But Natalie was very small and every extra pound showed. She would stand at the mirror and stretch her neck, striking one pose after another. Even walking down the street, she'd suddenly spot her reflection in a shop window and she'd straighten up her neck and keep walking.

"I'm fighting every damn one of them," she said as the years began to accumulate.

4

By 1954, the year she made *Rebel Without a Cause*, Natalie had won what we called the Great Dating Wars. She was sixteen, radiating life and energy, and she'd finally worn down Mother's resistance. After a fashion. She had also worn down Mother's resistance to education, and when she was not in studio school, she was at Van Nuys High School making good grades and friends by the dozens. She was famous, and she knew it. But she also knew how to handle it. She had the common sense to eschew putting on airs; consequently her fame did not intimidate or even incur the resentment of her classmates.

The fact that Dennis Hopper and Sal Mineo were among the young men swimming in our backyard pool, making games out of diving down and touching the tile mermaid on the bottom, did not seem at all unusual to either Natalie or me. Tab Hunter, who was then the teenage idol of America, was also around, courting Natalie, and he was the one my mother liked. The others she tolerated.

As long as Natalie's social life centered around our

home, everything was fine. Mother was always there, ever watchful. But when Natalie went out on a date and chose to ignore Mother's assigned curfew— nine-thirty on week nights and ten P.M. on weekends —all hell broke loose. Natalie would arrive home and the shouting would start. Natalie's willpower, dutifully suppressed for most of her girlhood, now asserted itself with a vengeance. It wasn't easy for her, and sometimes she would go to her bedroom in tears and shaking, but she held her own. I dreaded these scenes and would hide under the covers, my pillow wrapped tightly around my head. My father, who was usually reading a book and drinking, would occasionally interrupt and order the shouting to halt, but he too tended to steer clear.

Natalie also had a driver's license and a bright pink Ford Thunderbird, the kind with the removable top and the round portholes. She now drove herself to the studio, Mother right beside her, and on occasion she went by herself. But never at night. When she was about to start *Rebel*, there were lengthy night rehearsals in Nicholas Ray's hotel room at the Chateau Marmont. Mother would toss a pillow and a blanket into the backseat of her car, drive the three of us over the hill to the Marmont. While Natalie rehearsed, Mother and I would sit in the dark waiting for her. Finally I would crawl in the backseat and fall asleep.

One day Natalie was driving along Mulholland, on her way to Beverly Hills for an appointment at the dentist's, when the car spun out of control and collided with one of the wood-and-metal barriers along the dangerous curves on this spectacular hilly drive. A post shot through the window of the car and stopped inches short of Natalie's head. The police delivered a badly shaken Natalie home, and when Mother saw her she started screaming hysterically.

"Mother, I'm fine. Please stop screaming," Natalie said. Mother kept right on.

"Mother, I'm fine," she said again, taking her by the shoulders and forcing her to look directly into her face. Finally Natalie—who should have been the one being comforted—got angry. "The car's a mess, but I'm fine. The money will keep rolling in, Mom, so please keep quiet."

No accident could dampen Natalie's emerging sense of independence. She had the car repaired and within a few weeks was out on her own again.

Natalie's coming of age brought a big change in my life. As she struggled to break free from our mother, Mother turned her concentration on me. Pop had pretty much been the focus of the earliest years of my life, but now Mom started to assert her presence. I began working, small parts in television and in films. Walter Matthau, Jack Lemmon, Charlton Heston, and Howard Duff all played my father in various shows, including several *Playhouse 90*'s. John Frankenheimer was one of the first directors I clearly remember. I worked frequently in live television, and for a reason. I learned to read early and I was a fast study—I could memorize a small part quickly. I did not especially enjoy acting. I did it because it was expected of me.

Following *Rebel*, Natalie was cast as John Wayne's niece in *The Searchers*, directed by John Ford. The idea of working with John Wayne excited Natalie. When I tried out for the role of the young Natalie in the picture, I got excited too, but for me the thrill was the prospect of going on location with my sister and living together in close quarters for a number of weeks. I couldn't wait.

"What do you do in an audition?" I asked Natalie. "Did you ever go to one?"

"Once. My first picture. It's easy, Lana. Just smile, flirt, and make it seem as though you're eager to be liked. You can do that, can't you?"

"I think so." I didn't think so at all.

The day of my audition arrived. I was ushered into a room where I was introduced to John Ford and John Wayne. I curtsied, and Mr. Wayne, who knew how to win children to his side in an instant, began talking and put me immediately at ease. There was no reading, no test at all. Instead, Mr. Ford puffed on his cigar and watched as Mr. Wayne and I talked. Or rather, Mr. Wayne talked and I tried following Mother's advice to manage more than monosyllabic answers. Finally Mr. Ford spoke.

"Lift her up, please."

Mr. Wayne stood up—he seemed to extend farther toward the ceiling than anyone I had ever seen in my life—grinned, and rubbed his huge hands together.

Then he reached down, picked me up, and never once stopped smiling at me.

"That's fine, no problem at all," he finally said, putting me down. And that was it.

While the film was being shot, Mother, Natalie, and I lived upstairs over a trading post outside Flagstaff, Arizona. I shared one bedroom with Mom, and Natalie had the other one to herself. There was nothing but rolling sand and desert, and each night the Indians would build campfires, and eventually they would begin singing. I was fascinated by the Indian women, who wore layer upon layer of clothing, all full of silver buttons. It was extremely hot and dry and I heard that the women never took their clothing off and that whenever they wanted to change clothes they simply piled on another layer. They all looked like heavy women, but my theory was that they were actually small women buried inside mounds of clothing.

When the Indians began to sing at night I would get scared. Then Ward Bond was bitten by a scorpion and Natalie and I watched them drain the poison from the bite. We looked away, terrified that the same fate awaited us. I was also afraid to take a bath; when you turned on the tap, the water would come out as red and dirty as the desert sand. I was certain it would stain my skin. After all, Natalie's color had changed. She'd decided to get a tan in order to look more like an Indian and need less makeup. What Natalie got was a severe burn that held up production for several days while she was bathed and kept in bed.

Thereafter, everything went smoothly. Natalie developed a crush on Patrick Wayne, the second son of Mr. Wayne, and even I, who at the age of nine had no use whatsoever for boys, had to admit he was handsome. However, not as handsome or as exciting as his father. Mr. Wayne was popular with both the Indians and the children working on the film, and to all of us he passed out Allenberry pastilles, black-currant candies which darkened our tongues and gums and tasted like fresh fruit.

Once back in Los Angeles the subtle shifts in our lives continued. Instead of accompanying Natalie to the studio, Mother would now come along with me; by now I was working a lot of the time.

I was also in studio school with Portland Mason, James Mason's daughter, and she was in rehearsal for a *Playhouse 90*. I had just finished one show and would not begin rehearsing the next for a week, and so I plunged happily into schoolwork, burying myself in my books. Portland went on with her rehearsals, and the day before the play was to be shot live, Portland came down with chicken pox and I was rushed in to replace her.

For the first time in my life I not only noticed the pressures being placed upon me, I reacted to them. They started running me through the sets, showing me my marks, while an assistant director taught me the script. It was an afternoon of "This is where you sit, then you walk here, stop, turn and say this, then you leave through this door, quickly walk across to the other set and sit in that chair, because the cut is directly from you . . . to you.'' I listened, tried to learn my lines, then retreated to my dressing room, where I began sobbing. Mother soothed me, calmed me down, and bolstered my self-confidence. I thought I'd never get it right, and I was terrified.

Less than three hours after I had been thrown into Portland's role, the red spots began to emerge through my ample supply of freckles, and my fever began. Someone carried me to Mother's car, keeping me bundled in a blanket, and Mother tagged along apologizing to everyone for my illness. I have no idea what hapless child actor next came under pressure and acted out the part in a state of terror. I was sound asleep when the show aired the following day.

5

The stories Mother told were fascinating and at times frightening. She spun her tales depending upon the impact she wanted to achieve, and sometimes that impact was stunning. The first audience was Olga— whom Mother claimed as a witness for various adventures from her life in China, although Olga was at the time too young to remember much—and then Natalie and then me. Natalie and I heard the stories closer in time than Olga did, and as it turned out years later when we got together to compare notes, we all heard slightly different versions.

Mother's tales were elaborate and exotic, just as she herself seemed to me to be. She claimed, at times, to be the abandoned daughter of Gypsies, left on a Siberian hillside. This, she said, was one of the reasons she was able to read fortunes. She said she was found by another family and taken into their midst as one of their own. The family that took her in was grand and aristocratic, and they raised her among their own children.

It was also why she claimed to be something of a psychic. She told fortunes and made psychic predictions with a deck of cards. She would begin with a full deck and remove the twos, fives, jokers, and anything which she construed to be a wild card. The person whose fortune was being told would first have to establish contact with the cards and the fortune therein, either by holding them—which most people did—or by sitting on them, which the true believers did. Each person was assigned "his" card. Natalie and I were assigned the Queen of Clubs, the card for unmarried women with dark hair. Later, after Natalie was married, her card became the Queen of Spades. The telling of the fortune was a long process, involving the elimination of cards until, finally, the fortune could be told. First, the person made a wish, a wish that was not communicated to Mother. If the wish was to be granted, it was necessary that there be only seven cards left at the end of the reading. If there were more or fewer, the wish would not be granted. There were also predictions, based on the sorts of cards remaining at the end of the fortune-telling.

All this Mother claimed to have learned from the Gypsies, and her conviction about her knowledge was such that we both believed it; by the time Natalie was old enough to contest it, I was totally in its thrall. We learned our lessons: Do not walk under a ladder or allow a black cat to cross your path (if one crosses, turn back). We lived in a world where people knocked on wood and threw salt over their shoulders. One afternoon Natalie walked to an empty lot near our house with a broken mirror, throwing shards over her right shoulder to forestall bad luck. I still carefully walk around a pole on the same side as my companion; otherwise we'll have an argument. Natalie and I were grown women and mothers when we found ourselves dancing around a pole on Canon Drive in Beverly Hills to avoid taking opposite sides. We did our little shuffle before it occurred to us how ludicrous it all was and we broke up laughing. No matter the humor we later found in some of the superstitions taught, we still spent most of our adult lives afraid of arguments or confrontations of any sort.

I have no idea of the actual facts of my mother's early years, but I do have her stories and my own impressions. She was born Maria Kuleff in Tomsk, a city in Siberia, to a beautiful, aristocratic mother and a father not to the manor born. Her family owned a great deal of land, chocolate and candle factories, and many stores. Why my grandmother married a poor man has any number of explanations, all the way from passionate love to an arrangement necessitated by the complicated business affairs of the man who was my great-grandfather. It all depends on when the story is being told and under what circumstances.

This much seems certain: when the Russian revolution began, the family fled. Fled, that is, if Mother's story of a private train equipped with family, family treasures, and servants can be called fleeing. They traveled to Harbin, a city in northeastern China that was largely populated by Russian immigrants. It was a Chinese city so Russian that the stores, the streets, and the local language was largely Russian. There Mother's family settled into a life of leisure, but not for long. Eventually the family fortune dwindled and life began to change.

She describes herself as a strong-willed, independent child who would do anything necessary to have her own way. I believe her.

She cites an incident which took place soon after they moved to China as proof of her psychic powers. For many years, I believed this too. She says that her family moved into a luxurious house in Harbin across the street from another, even larger house. My mother, who was then four, insisted she had lived in the larger house during another life. She even claimed she could describe its rooms. My grandmother, in an attempt to calm her headstrong child, took her across the street, knocked on the door, and introduced herself to the owner, a grande dame. After my grandmother explained the problem, my mother proceeded to describe the neighbor's bedroom, its dimensions, its furniture, and even the angel painted on the ceiling. The old lady, speechless, led them upstairs to the bedroom, which, Mother said, was exactly as she had described it.

The family's altered economic circumstances soon changed the nature of all their lives. My mother, trained in the ballet, joined a dance company, where her dark good looks and slim figure soon gained her a following. She has said that in her youth her heart overruled her head, and it apparently did just that when a handsome Russian-Armenian appeared and she fell in love with him. She married him and quickly produced a daughter, my stepsister, Olga. He preceded his wife and daughter to America, and in 1930 they followed him to San Francisco. There she discovered, as the saying goes, he had made alternative arrangements.

Mother—with a small amount of help from her husband—counted her blessings and her money and found she had not much of either. No matter, she was determined to make her new life work. In a few years she met my father, married him, and in the first year of their marriage, had their first daughter, Natasha.

My father was a laborer and there never was much money. At Christmas Pop would walk into the hills around Santa Rosa, find a small fir or pine tree, chop it down, and carry it back to our house. Years later, when he was working in the studios, it was a source of pride for him to be able to afford to go down to a local vacant lot and buy a big Christmas tree for his family.

Throughout her life Mother has continued to tell fortunes. It is an elaborate process and it is done in Russian. Her ability to communicate the fortunes she tells has diminished with each child. Olga, who was born in China into a strictly Russian-speaking family, translated first and best. Natalie, whose Russian was nearly fluent, came next. Then me, by which time English had gained a firmer foothold in the house. Mother's fortunes required elaborate translation and she would often turn to me and begin firing away, and I would mumph around trying to find the closest

English word to match the Russian. It was not a very scientific process. By the time Natalie reached her teens—and her world by this time was considerably larger than any of ours—she began to dismiss Mother's fortunes.

"It's nonsense, Lana," Natalie patiently explained when she'd outgrown superstition and I was still gullible. "I mean, how can you really believe people's fate can be decided by some lady from Russia shuffling her cards around? My God, it's embarrassing. You've got to stop letting her tell your fortune."

I did not, at least not until I was fourteen. After that I began either leaving the room or asking her to stop when she began telling a fortune in my presence. At fourteen I had rarely been left alone and only then while Mom ran down to the market or went on a brief errand. One day, at the insistence of my friend Diane Price, Mother pulled out her deck of worn cards and proceeded to tell our fortunes. I translated, and the words I finally found predicted for the two of us "terrible bodily harm." That done, Mother was off on her errand and Diane and I were left alone in the house. We holed ourselves up in my bedroom and I swear, real or not, we heard somebody trying the door, we heard footsteps, we heard all the other things a fertile imagination can conjure up. We called Diane's father, and we called the police. Diane's dad arrived with a baseball bat, followed in short order by the police. We were certain we were about to be raped and mutilated, and we were nearly hysterical by the time they all arrived. Minutes later

Mother arrived and professed amazement at our hysteria. A skeptic, though not a very strong one, was born that day.

About our father's life I know less, but legend and fact are not mixed. He was born in Vladivostok into a poor family. They too fled the revolution—though certainly not in their own train—and went to Shanghai, where they once again faced poverty. One by one my father's parents sent their sons to Canada, dispersing them among relatives. My father went to an aunt and uncle who valued hard work but weren't keen to educate a nephew. My uncle Volodia found a job but also continued his education. He went on to considerable academic achievement and became a rocket scientist in northern California, and he is working still. Pop, who was also a good student, found work. During the years after high school he traveled from job to job, taking his beloved Russian books with him wherever he went. Eventually he landed in San Francisco.

His name at the time was Nicholai Zacharenko, but with the optimism of every other immigrant, he decided to Americanize his name. He changed it to Gurdin. It was, at the time, his idea of a good American name which still had slightly Russian reverberations. Many years later he would tell the story of his new name with a rueful smile, but he remained proud of it, too.

In 1937, when they met, our mother was an immigrant woman with a small daughter barely making do on the few dollars she received from her ex-husband.

She was living with her friend Nadia Ermolova, a fellow immigrant and a ballet teacher. Pop was a laborer, a man without much more than the clothes on his back and the books he kept at his side.

Russian families are known for their intimacy, their extreme closeness, and their intertwined destinies. Ours was not. Relatives from both sides of the family appeared from time to time, but never for long and never with satisfactory results. They would leave in the midst of unhappiness, acrimony, and disputes. For us, the extended family was only a dream, and when Hollywood entered our lives, it was gone for good except for those brief occasions like marriages and funerals when families, no matter what their grievances, gather.

Our mother was, it seemed from the perspective of childhood, dramatic and colorful. Pop, on the other hand, was aloof, distant, and, when he was home, absorbed in a book. I acquired my love of reading from him, but time and circumstance did not allow us to discover any other similarities. He was not an easy man, and his marriage was not a happy one. They bickered incessantly, and Mother's relentless drive clashed with his recalcitrant nature. As the years passed, the relationship deteriorated until Pop's dark, brooding Russian nature took over and he began to drink. When he didn't come home from work, Mother packed us into the car and we set off for the bars frequented by the studio workers. We found him and he returned with us, only to begin drinking in earnest as soon as he was home. Finally his frustration, his unhappiness, prevailed, and he erupted into violent rages, throwing china, smashing chairs, and sending Natalie and me for cover under our beds. These evenings, which occurred every three or four months, ended with Pop at home venting his considerable anger and the rest of us in a motel along Ventura Boulevard waiting out his anger. The morning after, he always went to work. He must have had great, epic hangovers, but he was also a conscientious man who never missed a day's work. We would wait until he was gone and return home and begin cleaning up the house.

He was a man with his own code of ethics, his own sense of morality, and if it struck others as odd, so be it. One day at the studio one of his co-workers walked by and playfully goosed my father. He was infuriated and warned that the next man who goosed him would get his arm broken. Bets were placed, practical jokes were planned, and finally one day Pop got goosed again. He made good on his threat.

It is often the nature of fathers and daughters to eventually accommodate themselves to their differences, to whatever in their personalities causes difficulties between them. Natalie was the first to form an unspoken but obvious bond with our father, to accept him as he was and to understand his nature. By this time she was well into her second marriage and had been in analysis for years; perhaps she had resolved her conflicts over their relationship. It was something we seldom discussed, for at the time I was in the throes of trying to control my own life, and generally making a mess of it. By the time I was ready to know him better and to understand, to forgive and to ask to be forgiven, he was gone.

To this day I am struck by the contrast between what I have been told, what I have seen, and what I know for certain. Of the latter there is little. I remember one day as a teenager coming across a box full of dusty family pictures and finding one of a stooped old woman dressed in ordinary clothing, a shawl wrapped around her shoulders, the troubles of the world traced across the lines of her grim countenance. My mother, then a young and attractive woman, stood beside her.

"Is this my grandmother?"

"Yes, that's her."

She looked neither exotic, nor aristocratic, nor beautiful. I stared at the picture, and in my mind there were many conflicting images.

"That was after the fortune was gone," my mother said, interpreting the look on my face. "Then, everything changed."

Natalie, too, tended to doubt the more colorful versions of our family history, but she soon learned they served a purpose.

"I let Mother do the talking," she explained to me when I asked her about all the stories, "and then I sit back and look exotic. It always works. Whoever she's telling the story to immediately looks to me as if that explains how I became a star. Don't ever take the mystery away from people. They thrive on their little mysteries and their dreams."

6

Natalie and I were discussing our childhood once and I described it as living so long in a house where the kitchen table had a red tablecloth on it that it came as a great shock to discover other people had blue tablecloths in their kitchen. Natalie laughed and agreed, and said that for all the freedom we seemed to others to have, we were actually kept on a very tight rein. We did not even have separate bedrooms until Natalie was well into her teens and we were living in Sherman Oaks in a house with a pool in the backyard. It was my cherished belief that some of the money I had earned acting went to pay for that pool. My income as a child actress didn't amount to enough to necessitate a trip to court to protect it, and I had no interest in money anyway.

Natalie did, or at least she became interested after she began to get some notion of the sums she was earning. She was never the highest-paid actress in Hollywood, but she was right up there. She would ask questions, questions which Mom sometimes answered and sometimes didn't. When Mom was evasive, Natalie would press. Then the truth would come out. Mom lived in fear of Natalie's disapproval—economic and otherwise—and would do nothing to irritate her. If Mom didn't know the answer, Natalie would call her agent or her business manager or her lawyer. For many years they treated her as a child—which she was—but even after she had become a young woman the attitude persisted. Natalie persisted too, and once her psychoanalysis was well under way and she began to take charge, those who did not treat her as she expected to be treated were summarily fired. One by one, all the people who had controlled Natalie's life were discharged and replaced by others who treated her as an adult.

Life magazine once did a spread on her, including a photograph of Natalie sitting at a conference table, the sort found in corporate boardrooms, surrounded by her lawyer, agent, press agent, and business manager. She kept a copy of the picture in her desk drawer and, one by one, each had a red X drawn through him after he was canned.

Natalie was never complacent about her acting. She was inquisitive and eager to learn, though she was untrained and totally instinctive, the sort of actress that only Hollywood can produce. Her childhood beauty opened doors, and first Mother's and then Natalie's drive took it from there. Acting was her life and she knew it.

I had little interest in acting myself. It was simply something that was expected of me. What I was really interested in was school, my own room, and my books. Nancy Drew and her friends George and Bess were my best friends. I read every Nancy Drew book twice. Even Natalie, who encouraged my interest in reading and school, teased me about my obsession. I so wanted to be Nancy Drew that when her stories became a television series some years later I nearly cried when I realized I was too old to play her.

School was the Dickens Street Elementary School in Sherman Oaks, within walking distance of our house. It took a great many years for me to socialize. In grammar school I was shy and sat in the back of the room and got good grades. I formed tentative friendships with other girls. Although sleeping over was very popular, I was not permitted to spend the night away from home. However, I would occasionally be allowed to have a friend over to spend the night with me. Some of the other kids in the school teased me and called me stuck-up because I had a famous sister. When this happened I'd run home in tears, swearing never to return to school.

I came racing home one day, my eyes and nose red from crying, threw my lunch pail on the kitchen counter, and, uncharacteristically for me, blurted out my problem and asked my parents to do something about it.

"There, Lana," my mother said. "I'll buy you a new dress tomorrow."

"I don't want a dress! I want somebody to talk to. Somebody to listen to my problems." I ran from the kitchen and spent the afternoon in my bedroom. My problems remained undiscussed and unsolved. We were not a communicative family, and the only person who responded to my troubles was Natalie, who by now was fully occupied with her own life—most of it being lived outside our home. Her career had evolved into a way of life—shooting films, doing interviews, and going to still-photo sessions and fittings—a movie star's hectic routine.

She had little time for me, but when we were together she was generous and loving. Natalie listened. When I'd finished my small litany of complaints, she'd speak.

"Lana, what you've got to do is stay in school, keep making good grades, and then you can do whatever you want. School is important. Don't worry about anything else. I'll always be here for you."

When she wasn't working, Natalie would leave the studio school and head for Van Nuys High School, where she had what she called her "other life." She liked school, had several girlfriends, and after school they'd come home with her and disappear into her room. Pretty soon rock 'n' roll—the earlier, purer kind—could be heard on her record player and there would be much giggling. I was dying of curiosity to know what was going on in her room, but I could not conceive of going up to the door and asking to come in.

There were things we did together, too. When *Giant* premiered, Natalie bought a breathtaking dress and Dennis Hopper was to be her date for the evening. My awe must have been pitifully transparent because before I knew it Natalie scooped me into her

Thunderbird and drove me to Beverly Hills. She bought me a new dress and on the night of the premiere, Dennis Hopper appeared at our door with his little brother, who was to be my date. I have a picture of the four of us and I remember exactly how I felt when it was taken. I knew now I would never be another Natalie, but I felt that she was an extension of me and that as long as she was near me everything would be all right. It was all the illusion of a little girl accustomed to illusion and not very good at sorting out what was real and what was not. I felt beautiful and loved because Natalie made me feel that way. No wonder I loved her so.

As much as I enjoyed school, there was a powerful lure drawing me away from it—Mother. Her involvement in my life continued to grow, and given her indifference toward school and her ability to impose her will on me, it was not all that difficult to talk me into playing hooky for a day of shopping or playing around the house with her as my companion. I both needed and liked her company and I knew it would please her if I stayed with her. Shopping held particular appeal—I was becoming a clothes horse early and the thought of a new dress, chosen for me by my mother, had me out the door ready to go in an instant.

After every day of hooky, and there would be as many as two or three in one week, Mother would write a note saying I had been sick; I'd dutifully drop the note on my teacher's desk when I returned. Before long a social worker appeared at our house to

complain that I was probably more truant than sick.
She had watched me at school and found me to be a
remarkably healthy child. There were laws about tru-
ancy, laws my mother was obligated to observe. My
school attendance improved immediately. My grades
never suffered anyway.

Natalie gave me a television set for my bedroom—
to me the height of luxury. I was not permitted to
watch it after bedtime; each night, eager to please,
I'd turn out the lights, get in bed, and turn on the
television without the sound. I had trouble figuring
out what was going on and had to watch *Dracula* three
times before the plot was clear to me. When I finally
was able to watch it sound on, I was surprised to
discover I preferred the silent version. It was more
exciting that way.

One day I was in my bedroom with a couple of
girlfriends. We were discussing the latest topic to
appear on our horizon: boys. We were also standing
in front of the mirror, slicking our bangs and trying
to look pretty. Mother overheard our conversation,
and after a few minutes of listening, came marching
purposefully into my room and asked my girlfriends
to step outside for a moment. She said she had something very important to discuss with me.

"So, you're talking about boys now. Do you know
about sex?"

"A little." Very little.

"You've seen how our dogs and cats breed?"

"Yes."

"Well, that's the way people do it too." With that,

she left. My girlfriends came back into the room and I told them what my mother had said. We had to hold pillows over our mouths to muffle our guffaws. This was the first we'd heard about sex, and canine coupling was to be the extent of Mother's instruction; it's amazing I didn't grow up with rug burns on my knees and elbows. I once asked Natalie if her introduction had been similarly informative.

"Nobody ever said a thing to me. I just assumed that's what the dogs were doing. But"—and then she stopped and studied me for a moment before deciding it was safe to come right out with it—"I learned early. There is a lot of talk about sex on movie sets. On some of them there's a lot more than talk."

"Were you a virgin when you met R.J.?"

That one she wasn't prepared for. She thought a second and said, "Pretty much."

On the subject of sex, as with many other things, Mother was nothing if not inconsistent. She was in some ways a very old-fashioned, traditional mother and in other ways a very modern one. When it came time for Natalie's sexual initiation—or at least what Mother thought was her initiation—it took place with Mother's full cooperation.

For all her resistance, all the shouting and yelling, Mother finally accepted boys as a major part of Natalie's life. When Natalie was dating Nicky Hilton, I saw them holding hands and stealing kisses as they played in the pool. I stayed out of the way as much as I could, but curiosity got the better of me and I found Natalie's billing and cooing with boyfriends so ro-

mantic that, while Natalie fell in and out of love, I fell
irrevocably in love with love. With certain exceptions. When Nicky ran down to the market to pick up
a loaf of bread Mother had forgotten to buy, I
jumped into the car with him, imagining myself to be
his date for the trip to the store. We were walking
down the aisle looking for the bread when a woman
walked by and said, "Oh, my, what a nice little girl. Is
this your daughter?" I nearly died of embarrassment.

Then came Natalie's abortive romance with Elvis
Presley. They met, and Elvis flew Natalie to his family
in Nashville.

They were to be gone almost a week, but just two
days into the great adventure, Natalie called.

"Gladys has wrecked everything," Natalie said, re-
ferring to Elvis' domineering, jealous mother. "I
don't have a chance. Get me out of this, and fast,"
Natalie said.

It was agreed that Mother would call Natalie back
and ask her to come home because of some family
emergency. Natalie's romance with the king of rock
fizzled out.

"God, it was awful," she told me later. "He can
sing, but he can't do much else."

In the midst of the dating game Natalie graduated
from Van Nuys High School, an accomplishment she
was particularly proud of. She had to take a day off
from the studio to graduate, and for once Mother
and the studio cooperated. Twentieth Century-Fox
saw a way to get some publicity out of the ceremony.
When Natalie marched up to receive her diploma, a

brace of photographers appeared and the flashbulbs started popping. Natalie had insisted the occasion be a private family event; now she burst into tears and left the auditorium.

After graduation there appeared at our house an impossibly handsome young man, as dark-haired as Natalie. When I saw them together and sensed romance in the air, my heart raced. Robert Wagner— R.J., as he wanted to be known—was nowhere near as big a star as Natalie. He had appeared in a few films, notably *Titanic* with Barbara Stanwyck and Clifton Webb, and then primarily as a pretty face with nothing much to do. He certainly had not yet arrived as an actor. But he was in love, and so was Natalie. This was the real thing.

Their courtship was conducted in public; wherever they went, photographers were not far behind. In the spring of 1957 Natalie was nineteen, a young woman who had made her way gracefully through adolescence—and constantly before a camera at that. Now she was in love.

Natalie, Mother, and I went to Schroon Lake in the Adiron-dacks, and we stayed in a great sprawling old hotel with a beach, boats, and an amphitheater. It was here that *Marjorie Morningstar* was shot, and it was here that Mother came to deal with the facts of Natalie's life.

We were no sooner in our suite, where I shared one bedroom with Mother, and Natalie had the other

to herself, than R.J. arrived and moved into Natalie's
bedroom. Mother, quietly accepting the inevitable
and trying to prove herself a liberal soul, served them
breakfast in bed.

7

On December 6, 1957, almost a year to the day after they'd first met, R.J. arrived at the house with a bottle of champagne and two crystal glasses. Just for a celebration, he told her, and when she drank hers, she found at the bottom of the glass a pearl-and-diamond ring.

"Read inside," he told her.

She held the ring closely and read the inscription inside. "MARRY ME" was what it said. Three weeks later, that is what she did. She told me how he'd proposed to her with diamonds and pearls, and I thought it was the most romantic, exciting thing I'd ever heard; though I feigned a swoon while she laughed at me, it was not as feigned as I made it appear.

Natalie—or Nate, as R.J. now called her—took me to the lady who was making her wedding dress and had me fitted for a white *peau de soie* dress, with tiny seed pearls sewn into it. She made me a matching hat, and when I put it all on for the final fitting, I felt pretty for the first time in my life. Neither Natalie, nor Mother, nor I noticed a crucial component to the dress was missing, and we didn't realize it until we were in Scottsdale, where R.J.'s parents lived, and it was too late.

I had no shoes to go with the dress. Mother rushed me out to the first store she could find, and she bought what I considered to be the ugliest pair of white shoes I had ever seen. It was the only pair in my size. At that age children tend to be very conscious of what clothes they're wearing, and because I was so thrilled with my *peau de soie* dress, I was even more humiliated. But, as Mother pointed out, it was Natalie's day and I was not to make a fuss. I swallowed my pride and stood at the altar beside Natalie.

The ceremony had just commenced when tears started rolling down my cheeks, and small hysterical sobs followed quickly. I was losing her. She wasn't going to live at home anymore. I didn't know when I'd see her again. Natalie was going away. This perfect person I wanted to be like wasn't going to be in my life anymore. The first person Natalie kissed after she kissed her husband was me. She took me into her arms and comforted me.

"Please don't go away from me. Please," I said, trying to stop my tears.

"I'll always be there for you. Never worry. And even if I'm not living at home anymore, you will come and stay with us sometimes."

"You promise?"

"I promise."

Many years had to pass before we would talk about

those days, before Natalie would tell me that the
young bride I idolized was not at all what she seemed
to me. She was frightened, insecure, terrified she
would not meet her obligations to all the people who
surrounded her, unable to sleep at night, and except
for the early years of her marriage, desperately unhappy. So much so she began taking sleeping pills at
night. And finally, she sought professional help—
over her husband's objections. When she told me all
of this, I was able to understand and support her in
return. Had she told me any of this at the time of her
marriage, I don't know what I would have done. I was
prepared to believe anything she told me, but I don't
know if I would have been able to accept the truth. I
was too young to be able to believe her life was
different than I imagined it. I was, after all, wishing
upon a star.

Natalie was afraid of flying; she and R.J. went to
Florida on their honeymoon by train. R.J. allowed a
photographer he knew to take pictures of their jour-
ney with the understanding that the pictures were
private and not to be shown to anyone. Fat chance.
The photographer sold the pictures and by the time
Natalie and R.J. were back from their honeymoon the
pictures were appearing in all the fan magazines.
Natalie, whose sense of privacy had become even
more important to her since the incident at her high-
school graduation, felt violated. R.J. felt betrayed by
a friend. It was an incident which would be repeated
at their next marriage, too, creating ill feelings which
I regret to say I think never were assuaged.

As Natalie and R.J. settled into their life together, I settled into a life pretty much without Natalie and very much with Mother. It seems to me now that the harder Natalie pushed Mother out of her life, the more she became involved with mine. Over my protests my career was activated again, a move which met with only marginal success because I was a gangly child verging on my teens and in a great rush to get there. To put flesh on my bones I drank Weight-On by the bottle. I was not quite the stuff for stardom. Mother insisted that, as she put it, "The camera likes you," and I must say she had a point. I photographed better than I thought I looked, but I still didn't work a whole lot.

We were walking down the street one afternoon and we happened to pass a particularly homely little girl who was walking with her mother. Mother looked at the girl and, once we were safely past, whispered to me: "If I had a child that ugly I'd drown her." I felt I wasn't much better-looking. This remark by my mother would come to be a familiar refrain to my therapists and psychiatrists in the years to come. I had to be beautiful if only to please my mother.

Natalie and R.J. bought a house in Beverly Hills, and Natalie, in a fit of creativity, decided to remodel it. For weeks walls were torn out, rooms rearranged, and Natalie would rush off to furniture stores and buy like mad. The result was one of those white-and-gold houses for which Beverly Hills and Hollywood are notorious. The house—and Natalie's decorating abilities—became something of a gentle joke. The result was not lost on Natalie, either, who thereafter sought advice from professionals when she was decorating a home. But the first house became an albatross, and it was quite some time after her divorce before a buyer could be found for the white-and-gold elephant.

There was one thing she always kept with her—through her marriages to R.J. and Richard Gregson. It was a bust of James Dean that someone had given her, and it was for many years one of her prize possessions, a touchstone to another time. The last I saw of it, it was sitting in a place of honor in a big pine étagère in her living room when she was married to Richard. No one has seen it since, and I'm sure it's packed away somewhere, because she swore she'd never part with it.

I went to Van Nuys Junior High School and began to emerge from my shell of shyness. Natalie later said I didn't so much emerge as propel myself to the opposite extreme. I became outgoing, articulate, and came to consider myself a great wit, a claim that was certainly open to dispute. It took several years for all of this to happen, but it was a period of growth enforced upon me by myself and I found the experience enhancing in every way. I had also begun to mature physically and I did anything I could to keep the boys from staring at my breasts, even to sitting at my desk stoop-shouldered, trying to hide them. I had worn a bra since the fifth grade, but by now they were far too big to be hidden by a bra.

I formed friendships, some of which survive to the

present. I also had my first crush; I look upon it now as thoroughly consistent with my inability at the time to tell the difference between fantasy and reality. My crush was on Peter Pan. I owned every Peter Pan comic book that had been printed and I kept them stacked in order in a box under my bed. I wanted to live forever with him in Never-Never-Land; sometimes I still want to. When I took my own daughter on the Peter Pan ride to Never-Never-Land at Disneyland, it was not little Evan who emerged wide-eyed and dreamlike. My crush remained private until a girlfriend came over and unearthed my stash of comic books under the bed. I started crying because my secret was exposed and because somebody else was looking at my Peter Pan.

I was fourteen when I was cast in *Five Finger Exercise*, a melodrama which was about . . . about two hours long. It starred Rosalind Russell, Maximilian Schell, and Richard Beymer. Max played a piano teacher for the little girl of the family. I'm her chum. She sort of falls in love with him. So does Roz. Dick, as my girlfriend's older brother, has a great crisis because he can't identify with his father but there is this wonderful piano teacher to talk to. That sort of stuff.

I bit my nails, and in order to get me to stop, Mother promised me a ring. My prize was a gold ring with two little diamonds on the edge of it, set in a sort of sweeping design. I thought it was incredibly special and between takes of *Five Finger Exercise* I would stand and look at it and my nice long nails. In one scene I had to go into the surf in Santa Monica, and I worried I might lose my ring. On that particular day Mother was busy elsewhere and recruited a friend, an eighteen-year-old boy named Gary Patterson, now a successful illustrator, to chaperon me on the set as required by law. Gary had gone off somewhere looking at the girls when it came time for me to take the plunge, and Maximilian Schell stepped forward and offered to keep my ring for me.

I did the scene in two takes and then went to him to get my ring back. He held it in his hand, looked at it, then put it in his pocket and took my hand in his.

"I'll only give it back to you if you go out with me." I was sure he was joking, but I didn't wait around to find out.

I went home in tears, terrified of telling Mother what had happened, even more terrified of what it was I might have to do to get my ring back. The following day, he repeated his condition, and that night, desperate, I called Natalie.

"He what?"

I repeated my tale of woe, and then there was a brief silence while Natalie contemplated what to do.

"You just do your job and stay out of the way of that son-of-a-bitch," she said. I was startled, because swearing was something I never heard from Natalie. "I'll get your ring back."

There is nothing quite so effective as an indignant older sister. Natalie sprang into action, Schell didn't speak to me again for the two remaining days left on the picture. He didn't return my ring, either. He

waited until he was back home in Germany and
mailed it to me. In a regular plain white envelope.

We did not meet again until I was in my mid-twen-
ties, unmarried for the moment. He asked me for a
date and I accepted out of curiosity to see if the
subject of the ring would come up. It didn't. I found
him boring and did not see him again. It would have
given me a certain pleasure to withhold from him
once again what it was he was after, but in truth the
subject never came up the second time we met.

The experience did serve to diminish even further
my already attenuated interest in an acting career.
Mom—I was a teenager now and she had ceased to
be called Mother—was as relentless as ever about my
career. She pushed, I resisted.

When push finally came to shove, I ran away from
home.

8

The term "stage mother" evokes certain images, most of them based on the overpowering, overambitious mother in *Gypsy*, played on Broadway by Ethel Merman and on the screen by Rosalind Russell, with Natalie portraying Gypsy Rose Lee in the latter version—at the time to a barrage of jokes between the two of us. It seems to me the point in *Gypsy* and also in all stories of stage mothers is that the mother does not truly understand that along with creating success she may be causing damage. If it was possible to get this across, I think stage mothers would moderate their ambitions for their children. Their destructive drive comes from a desperate effort to escape a life they find oppressive and unhappy. History is crammed with stories of the oppressed quickly turning into the oppressors.

I have tried from time to time to discuss all this with Mom. I have only to mention the term "stage mother"—a term which would send most mothers into a fury of self-righteous defense—and Mom will smile.

"Yes! That's right! I pushed and I argued and I once even talked to Jack Warner, went in and fought with him, and I made sure Natalie got what she wanted."

Mom is very proud of that. She is not proud of her involvement in my career, because it did not go her way, she was never in command for long, and I did not become a star. She believes if I had done as she told me to do, I would be a star today. It is a subject we no longer discuss.

To her credit, she certainly tried hard. When I was in junior high school, happy with my friends, my classes, and, finally, the occasional boyfriend, she'd announce over breakfast that I'd be leaving school early that day to go to an audition. I went a couple of times, and each time I'd return home in tears, wringing my hands, my stomach upset. I was frightened of being examined by a table full of men, reading a script to them, smiling, and doing the curtsy Mom demanded (when Mom wasn't in the room, which was more often than not, I skipped the curtsy). I was also afraid of being rejected.

When I balked, she cajoled me. She told me about all the advantages there'd be in doing that particular role. She pointed out the fun and the glamour and mentioned how envious other children would be of my good fortune. She was calm, quiet, and persuasive, and she always made her point. She also had a trump card she knew would bring me around every time: if I didn't do this, I would never have a chance to be anything like Natalie. I was easily swayed. I wanted to please my mother and be acceptable to her. The fear of rejection by the people who were auditioning me remained, but it was not as great as my fear of losing Mother's love.

Meanwhile, I had graduated from my infatuation with Peter Pan and had fallen—hard—for James Bond. I read all of Ian Fleming and could recite nearly every exploit of Agent 007. I was also fascinated by the sex—restrained as it was—in the books. I was definitely growing up.

Reading distracted me from my conflicts with Mom and guaranteed a happy ending. In my imagination, I was always part of the story. But eventually it would take more than escapist reading to extricate me from my problems at home. One morning Mom announced she would be taking me out of school at eleven and that I'd be spending the day auditioning for a big part. She told me the name of the film and the amount of time—two months—we'd be away on location. She promised I had a very good chance of getting the part. Only two others were being auditioned. She was brimming with optimism. I was paralyzed with fear. I have no memory of the name of the film, I remember only nodding at Mom, walking out of the house, and going to school. By the time I arrived, I was hysterical. I could not control my crying, my fear, or my anger. I did the only thing I could think to do. I called Natalie.

It was early and I woke them up. R.J. answered, listened for a moment, and then handed the phone to Natalie. I tried to tell her everything, but I must have

been incoherent, because she kept asking me to repeat things, and I sensed that she too was becoming
upset, because I could hear R.J. trying to calm her. I
finally conveyed that I did not want to go to the
audition, and that if Mom insisted, I was running
away.

Half an hour later, R.J. picked me up at school and
drove me across Coldwater Canyon and down Beverly Drive to their house. Natalie was waiting at the
door. She took me into her arms and I began sobbing. She could be the most loving person when she
wanted, but she had never been like this before.
While I believed she was living in Beverly Hills, happily married and oblivious of my troubles, she had in
fact been very well aware of all that was happening to
me. Mom had complained—frequently and at length
—about my lack of interest in acting, and had even
asked Natalie to intervene and encourage me. Natalie had refused. Now, faced with a crisis, Natalie had
made her move. I learned later that while R.J. had
come to pick me up, Natalie had called Mom and told
her what had happened. Mom had been furious, and
that strengthened Natalie's resolve. Natalie was now
in control, and Mom did as Natalie demanded.

The afternoon after I arrived, Natalie came into
the living room, sat down on the edge of her white-
and-gold sofa, and launched right into her plan of
action:

"Here's what I'm going to do. I will let you stay
here as long as it's necessary. I don't want her running your life the way she's doing it or taking out all

of her frustration on you. You realize that's what it is, don't you? She doesn't have me around anymore, so now she's going to turn you into a star. Even if you don't want it."

"Did you want to be a star?"

"Lana, I was too young for it to even occur to me I might have a choice. You're not."

By this time Natalie was in the early stages of what was to become a long and, for her, rewarding psycho-analysis. It was a complicated and confusing time in her life, and she later told me that once she saw an issue or a problem clearly stated—and mine was certainly clear enough—she'd move on it, move fast, because that way she could also avoid having to deal with what was less clear to her. She perceived my plight and had the courage and compassion to take bold actions to alleviate it.

She also made plans in the short time it took R.J. to bring me home. I was going to stay with them for a week or two and we would discuss everything. If I wanted to go to school, she would arrange for me to be driven over the hill to the Valley and back every day. I did not have to go home unless I wanted to go, and she promised me Mom would no longer push for an acting career. I must have looked very skeptical at this, but Natalie, looking me directly in the eye, her hands on my shoulders, swore it was so.

Her nurturing, her protection, was complete. That night she tucked me into her side of her bed, and she got into the middle next to R.J., who muttered a small protest but quickly gave in to Natalie's wish. It had long been the custom in our family that whenever one of us was sick or upset, the other would stay in bed until sleep came. Mom sometimes did this as well, and Natalie and I have done it with our daughters also. That I was landing on one side of a marriage bed did not seem, at the time, to make much difference, and I suspect that, with the possible exception of R.J., it didn't make any difference to Natalie either. One night R.J. objected.

"R.J., please. She's upset. It's only for a couple of nights and then she'll move into her own room."

I slept in their bed two or three nights before moving into their guest room, which Natalie, with typical thoroughness, had made over into a room perfectly suited for a teenage girl, complete with a small stereo set.

I did not go back to school, but I did proceed with my school-work. My decision was that I did not want any of my friends to discover what was going on. R.J. set out to find schools near their house, private schools where I would be given the support and encouragement he and Natalie believed I needed. The subject of boarding schools also came up, and R.J., who favored them, checked several of them out. I did not relish the idea of boarding school, but I was prepared to go if that was the only way to avoid acting.

I spent my days reading, either at the studio with Natalie or at their home. I listened to records and played with Conroy, their Labrador retriever, who always had an upset stomach from drinking the pool water and whose bad breath was infamous among Natalie and R.J.'s friends. For several days I did not receive a telephone call from Mom, nor did I hear Natalie speaking with her.

That, it turned out, was by design. Natalie spoke to Mom daily. What I did not know was that Natalie had not only supported my decision, she had done so with what turned out to be the most effective threat of all. She had said to Mom that if she ever asked me to go to another audition, she would pack me up and move me in with her and R.J. permanently. The push for the acting career was over. Or else. There would be no conditions, and no further negotiating.

Mom had no choice. She had long since given in to Natalie, had learned to bend to her will without protest. It must have been devastating to have her youngest daughter in revolt and to have such a powerful ally, but Mom accepted Natalie's ultimatum. When it was all over Natalie came into my bedroom and sat down on the edge of the bed.

"If you want, you can go back to Mom and Dad. She'll never ask you to go to an audition again. Or, if you want, you can stay here with us."

"Never?"

"Never. And if she ever asks you again, call me up and we'll come and get you."

I went home. It took some time for me to learn the story of all that had happened, and when I did I also began to understand a subtle change that had taken place in my life within the Gurdin family. In Mom's eyes I was a failure. I was forgiven, but I was a failure.

9

From time to time I went to Natalie and R.J.'s for a weekend, or we'd all be invited over for dinner. Natalie's invitations had one eccentric quality to them: they were never for noon, or five, or any hour or half-hour. Natalie's invitations were for 1:10 or 5:20 or some other odd time. This was a habit begun shortly after Natalie married and began life on her own, and it was one that continued up to the end of her life—at least so far as her family was concerned. At first there would be a mad rush so that Pop, Mom, and I would arrive exactly on time. Sometimes we'd arrive early and park a block away to await the appropriate time. Mom in particular was always afraid she'd be late. It made no difference, really, because no matter what time we'd arrive, Natalie would not be ready. Natalie at work was punctual and prepared. Natalie at home had a very fanciful sense of time.

On the weekends I spent with her, Natalie and I became sisters again, sitting at her makeup table experimenting with cosmetics, and I would try on her clothes. Whenever I put on something I especially liked or she thought was right for me, she'd give it to me with a wave of her arm. We'd primp and play for hours, while R.J. would wait impatiently for Natalie to get ready. Then they'd go out to their party and I'd go off to mine. Curfews, which had been such a big part of Natalie's life, were not a consideration in mine. Mom had placed none on me and Natalie never even mentioned the matter. I was seldom out too late anyway—especially when I was staying with Natalie. I wanted to get home and hear all about where she'd been.

Her therapy was now the most important activity in her life. She went every day, and when she was working she would either get two hours off for the short drive from the studio to her analyst or she would retreat to her dressing room and have her session by telephone. I say it was the most important thing in her life from a perspective of time, for I was unaware that her marriage was not working and that, though they still loved one another very much, it was not enough. What specifics caused it to end—or even if there were specifics—I do not know. I do know that Natalie was going from one major film to another, while R.J. was still trying to get a successful career going. One of the best films she made during this time was *Splendor in the Grass*, and it was on this film that Warren Beatty came into her life.

So did Elia Kazan, and it was Gadge she fell in love with first, a love very different from the love she would come to feel for Warren. Gadge, as everybody called Kazan, was a director who came from the theater, a serious intellectual man who exuded a caressing warmth. Natalie, who was not a trained actress, was at first very intimidated about working with him. But she was an actress who flowed with her instinct, and her instinct about him was strong and trusting. Their collaboration was such a success it brought her a second Academy Award nomination. The first had been as Best Supporting Actress in *Rebel Without a Cause*. This time it would be for Best Actress.

I was hanging around the set when Natalie's trouble with tears reappeared. She was to cry in a scene and she didn't think she could do it. She appealed to Gadge. Speaking in a quiet voice, she kept repeating, "Gadge, I just don't think I can do it. I'm afraid." He heard her out and then called over Barbara Loden, who was also in the picture.

"Barbara, would you cry for us, please?"

Barbara put her head down and placed her hand over her eyes. When she looked up less than a minute later, tears were streaming down her cheeks. Natalie and I both looked on, astonished.

"How do you feel about that, Natalie?" he asked her.

"It's incredible. I'm so impressed. I'm so jealous," Natalie stammered.

"No, no that's not what I meant. How did you feel?"

Natalie thought for a moment and came up with the right answer. "I was in awe of her for being able to do that. But I wasn't moved. Not at all."

"Exactly. Barbara can do it in an instant. She has a special ability. But she was just doing it, just showing you. There was no emotion involved. As long as you are honest with yourself, as long as you show genuine emotion, it won't matter if there are tears or not. The scene calls for you to show pain, not necessarily tears. Show pain, Natalie, and if it is real it will be all that is needed."

Natalie excused herself and went alone to her dressing room. Several minutes later the assistant director called her to shoot the scene. Natalie, looking unchanged, emerged and walked onto the set, found her marks, and put her head down in concentration. When Gadge called for action, he got it.

Natalie's look of pain was genuine, and so were the tears that followed. When the scene was done, the applause from the crew was genuine too, and when Gadge took her into his arms to compliment her, she buried her head on his shoulder and wept.

I do not know which came first, the end of her marriage or Warren Beatty, though I suspect—now that I know Warren—he might have precipitated the end of a deteriorating situation. Warren is nothing if not charming and insistent. He is accustomed to having his way. All I know is that one day Natalie, weeping, her hand bleeding because she had squeezed and broken one of her cherished crystal wineglasses, arrived at our house to tell us that R.J. was moving out and that the marriage was over.

I was shattered. Those two perfect people were no longer together, and though I could see that Natalie was deeply upset, I also believed that R.J. at that moment was probably in equally bad shape. Mom was furious and immediately cast R.J. as the villain, despite Natalie's insistence that it simply wasn't so.

Their separation and subsequent divorce in 1962 stunned Hollywood. It seemed as though everyone in the business had made them a symbol of their own private fantasies of perfection and of happily-ever-after. Elizabeth Taylor, the only other actress to successfully negotiate the treacherous shoals of going from child actress to adult star, was so miserable she later told Natalie she had to take a tranquilizer and go to bed. She had, she said, convinced herself that Natalie was going to do what Elizabeth had been unable to do: marry, have a family, a career, and stay married. As it turned out, Natalie couldn't either. Not yet.

When Natalie made a break, she made it fast and neat. But it took a while to unload her experiment in home decoration. She rented a house in Bel Air, one with a gigantic tree in the front yard where I would sit for hours, holding my breath as long as I could, afraid of startling the deer which used to come to feed on the shrubs around the tree.

When she tired of living in Bel Air, she rented another house, this one in Benedict Canyon. It had a big outdoor fountain and waterfall which turned into a stream running through the house, a stream which bred mosquitoes faster than the exterminator could get rid of them. R.J.'s name was seldom if ever mentioned as she went about her life. He was placed firmly and forever in the past—or so we all, including

Natalie, believed. If it was not really so in her heart, she willed it to be so in her mind.

Her romance with Warren Beatty became public. Together in public, they were something to behold: beautiful, exciting, sophisticated. Together, in private, they were in the midst of a tumultuous love affair. It became so intense that Warren, who had a reputation for maintaining both a separate identity as well as a separate residence, moved into Natalie's house.

Warren, as someone later remarked, was not yet Warren when he met Natalie. *Splendor in the Grass* had been his first film, but it had made him a star. *Bonnie and Clyde*, and the accumulation of his great power and wealth, were still years away. He was just beginning to learn his way around the business, to experiment with his career. His dreams were taking shape. He talked often about his desire to direct and produce, and Natalie always listened patiently. I don't think either of them had any inkling of the success that awaited Warren.

There was no question that they were in love, though at times it seemed to me the one more stricken was Natalie, but I quickly put my worries aside. Mom too was worried for her, but for different reasons—she knew about Warren's reputation for wandering, and at the time, I did not.

I was spending the week with Natalie and we were trying on clothes and having a great time. After a few hours I noticed she began to look at her watch, and by that evening she became distraught and finally began crying. I demanded she tell me what was bothering her, but she refused until, after one particularly urgent request by me, she stammered, "Warren." Later that night, hours after he had said he would be home and several hours after they had been due to arrive at a dinner party, Warren sauntered in. Then it started. Natalie and Warren fought, and when the screaming became too much, Warren slammed the door and left again and did not return that night. Natalie, weeping, went to bed, and I could not console her. She found it hard enough to admit to herself what was going on, harder still to explain it to a little sister who idolized her.

And who, in her fashion, defended her. Whenever Warren made Natalie unhappy, I became sullen and difficult. One night after a particularly big argument I proceeded to snap at Warren every time we spoke. Finally Natalie intervened and ordered me to apologize.

"For what? For the way he treats you?" I shot back.

"To be polite, Lana," she said evenly.

I stormed off to my room and slammed the door. Natalie followed, with Warren standing behind her, knocked, and ordered me to apologize. I refused. Finally I asked why.

"He's older than you, that's why."

I had expected her to say something like "For me. Do it for me," and I knew if she had I'd have done exactly as she wished. But I was unprepared for this and so I opened the door and yelled at Natalie, "Only chronologically!"

I then slammed the door as hard as I could.

10

While Natalie Wood and Warren Beatty were together they tended to live very privately. They occasionally had friends to dinner, but more often than not it was Natalie and Warren and, on weekends, just the three of us. It seemed to me that whenever Warren was in one room, Natalie was in another. Natalie would lie by the pool in the sun for an hour and then when Warren would appear in his trunks, his usual book tucked under his arm, she would get up and go into the house. It wasn't hostility, it certainly wasn't disinterest, and I have since come to think of it as two lives coming together briefly, but always at cross-purposes. There was always a distance between them.

When they did go out, Natalie would spend hours getting ready. Warren, who seemed always to wear the same outfit—an open, loose shirt and gabardine slacks—would wander around for a while, then go to the piano and play, sometimes for hours on end. He was silent, studious, he had a good sense of humor, and I knew that on most occasions he tolerated my presence.

If there is ever a film made about a man who loves women, but not well or truly enough, I hope Warren will make it. It is a story he knows well. He and Natalie were together slightly more than a year, and it was a time mixed with great highs of love and great lows. The lows came because of Warren's wandering eye. Warren does not believe he knows a woman until she has been in his bed, and Warren now knows a great many women—most of them beautiful and famous. Sexual fidelity isn't in Warren's vocabulary or his philosophy.

His constant search for candidates eventually fell on me. I was sixteen and no longer a scrawny little girl. On the contrary. I was also sophisticated beyond my age, but in some areas I was also naive. From time to time I would catch him watching me, his gaze open, interested, and inviting. I did not—at first—understand this and would retreat, giggling usually, to another room. But I understood all too well a year later, after he and Natalie had broken up and we all found ourselves reunited in a restaurant in New York.

Natalie had to go to New York for interviews and a round of other publicity chores. She invited me to come along, promising we'd have time to do some sightseeing and shopping. I couldn't wait.

We did all that and more. I got a suitcase full of new clothes, we went to the top of the Empire State Building, took a ride on the Staten Island ferry, and toured all the famous nightclubs. On one of our last nights there, we had a surprise visitor. Warren called and invited us to dinner. We had already made plans to eat with Tommy Thompson, a writer for *Life* magazine with whom Natalie was having a brief affair that would evolve into a lifelong friendship. Natalie invited Warren to join us. She didn't look happy at the prospect of being with Warren, but she was too polite to refuse. Saying no to Warren is not easy. We had no sooner started dinner than we all wished Natalie had said no. Natalie and Warren disagreed about nearly everything that night, not loudly but in sullen silence. Natalie, to her credit, put on a good performance, trying in between silences to be talkative and charming. Finally she excused herself, pleading fatigue and a long schedule the next morning. She and Tommy went back to the suite we were sharing after insisting that I stay with Warren.

Warren made his move. I was so astonished I reacted by giggling and pretending it was all a joke. It was not. Warren suggested we go to my hotel room. He told me I was always provoking him by running around Natalie's house in a bathing suit, that even though I pretended not to know what was happening I knew exactly what the score was. I smiled sweetly—and insincerely—and said it couldn't be so because I was never interested in him and, in fact, considered him the cause of much of my sister's unhappiness.

I was so far out of my league that I can honestly say I wasn't even sure what the game being played was. I just knew I was in big trouble. I had no money and no way of getting back to my hotel, and so I asked him to take me back. He was staying there too, as my luck would have it, and I suddenly realized I was trapped. I desperately fumbled for a way out, and as we walked into the lobby of the hotel, I looked around and in an instant knew exactly what to do.

"You go get my key, Warren, I'll wait here," I said, pretending to be embarrassed. He walked off to get it and I turned and ran across the lobby to the house phone. I called Natalie and woke her up.

"Hi! We're back! I left my key in the room. Open the door, will you?" I pretended to be very giddy, maybe even a tiny bit drunk, though I had not had a drop. By this time Warren had the key and was standing right in front of me, glaring. "I'm on my way up right now," I said into the phone.

"I can't, Warren. I'm very sorry, but I just can't," I said when I hung up. I could not conceive of doing anything to hurt Natalie, and even if she never found out, I would believe I had hurt her anyway. Nor did I wish to create an enemy out of Warren. Natalie's life was complicated enough; she didn't need any new source of trouble with Warren.

He was gracious about it, and I secretly think he admired me for my clever move. If he did, he never said so, but for the rest of the trip it was as though nothing had happened. Years later Warren would have his way, but not now.

When Warren went out of Natalie's life it was with the same finality, the same ferocity with which the marriage to R.J. ended. When Natalie decided to do something, it was done. Never mind that she was the injured party—she kept her sadness and her tears to herself. Life would go on, and if there was a grim determination about it, there was also a great deal of time and effort put into making it all work well again. Natalie was learning to manage her life and her career, and it wasn't easy.

11

While Natalie was struggling to take control of her life, I was losing control of mine, and though I tried to make things right, I failed miserably. The halcyon days at North Hollywood High School came to an abrupt end when Mom got a telephone call from the school confronting her with the fact we were using a false address for me, that of a friend who lived in the North Hollywood district. Somebody had turned me in. I left North Hollywood High and went to Ulysses S. Grant High School, North Hollywood's sworn enemy and a place where I knew absolutely no one.

I was miserable. It seemed to me I had always lived in two worlds: one, Natalie's, where everyone was older, sophisticated, and successful; and two, the typical world inhabited by high-school students. I had always tended to be more comfortable in the former and less at home in the latter. Now I reversed my preferences and I couldn't wait to turn sixteen, to have a driver's license, a car, and freedom. I remembered Natalie's monumental effort to gain independence and I anticipated I would have to do much the same.

Natalie, for her part, was more than ready to help. For my sixteenth birthday I had narrowed my choice down to two dresses and I couldn't make up my mind which one I wanted. In the course of a telephone conversation Mom joked with Natalie that I was about to expire from the process of decision-making. The next day, both dresses arrived at the house. I spread them out on top of my bed and thought they were the most beautiful dresses I had ever seen.

That was just the beginning of Natalie's largess. On my birthday I was given a Jaguar XKE convertible. All gold. It was an excessive gift for a young woman, but it was given out of an excess of love and Natalie's inability to distinguish between what was expensive and what was not. I was thrilled. Even Pop, who normally had little to say about fancy doings, became enthusiastic and took me out riding in my new car.

All of these grand gestures—including presents from Mom and Pop—cheered me up. I had gone from being a giggly chatterbox who was an excellent student to a quiet, sullen girl whose grades were slipping fast and who would spend hours on the telephone maneuvering her way into parties with various of Natalie's friends. Natalie, eager for me to have friends, often included me when she went out to parties, though by now her friends tended to be older and more established than her contemporaries.

As soon as I could drive I began hanging out with a crowd of actors and the offspring of prominent people, most of them older than I. Dack Rambo, who is now part of the drama of *All My Children*, was one; so was Cheryl Holdridge, a beautiful girl who later married Lance Reventlow, who was also part of this crowd. It was a fast track for me, and I gave it my all. One night at a party I met Jack Wrather III, the son of Jack Wrather, the businessman who owns a production company, the Disneyland Hotel, and several other major businesses, and the stepson of Bonita Granville Wrather. Jack was handsome and intense, only two years older than I but more worldly by far.

What first brought us together was a mutual sense of isolation, of being apart from the world in which we lived. He had had an unhappy childhood, his parents were divorced and at odds over how he was to be raised, and, like me, he seemed to spend most of his life trying to find firm footing on shifting ground, never sure where—or how—to step next. We began dating and were soon inseparable. I thought nothing of skipping school to go to the beach with him, and he would drop everything and come whenever I'd call and say I was depressed or lonely. We honestly believed we could rescue one another from our past and our respective unhappinesses.

When it came to independence, the rules that had applied to Natalie did not apply to me at all. Each time I'd stretch the boundaries I'd wait for some repercussion, and each time, there was nothing. I had no curfew. There were no guidelines. I was, without knowing it was so, on my own. I knew it for certain the day I came home and told Mom and Pop —I waited to make certain he was there just in case Mom exploded—that Jack and I were thinking of getting married. "Thinking" was the word I used for their benefit. We had already decided to get married. Right away. There was no objection from either Mom or Pop. Mom, in fact, seemed pleased by the idea. Natalie was off in Europe and knew nothing about it.

Mom stood in the driveway and waved good-bye when Jack and I drove off to be married in Tijuana, just the two of us with no attendants, no family to watch the ceremony. Jack wanted it that way and I was eager to please him. I was sixteen, he was eighteen, and to say we were inexperienced is to understate the case. We were not only sexually inexperienced, we had no real knowledge of relationships, of partnerships, or of any of the other things one is supposed to either bring to a marriage or learn about during its early years.

We were no sooner married than the pressures began to mount. We had no money, no jobs, nothing. We moved into a spare bedroom at Natalie's; she was living alone and insisted she welcomed the company. She seemed to be of two minds about the marriage: happy for me, but also with an unstated reservation. While we were driving along Sunset Boulevard on our way to go shopping, Natalie seemed strangely pensive. Finally she turned to me, and when she spoke, it was not the Natalie I imagined I knew so well:

"If you have a baby before I do, I'll just die."

I didn't know what to say and so I said nothing. In the next weeks nothing seemed to go right for us. Jack, even more accustomed to a certain style of living than I was, turned even moodier. One night, a little less than a month after we were married, he walked into our bedroom in a dark, angry mood and I made the mistake of complaining that he was late. He hit me. Then he hit me again, and started yelling. I was involved with a troubled man. And I'm not sure how much less troubled I was at the time. I knew only one thing for certain: I had made a bad mistake. But I was afraid to say so.

It didn't take Natalie long to figure out what was going on and she confronted me almost immediately. I became hysterical, more out of relief than fear, because on one level I had refused to admit to myself some sort of failure on my part. Jack's family was told of the fiasco, and so were Mom and Pop. Mom's official explanation to the Wrather family was that she had encouraged the marriage because she had caught us in bed together. She hadn't—Jack and I were so old-fashioned we didn't even go to bed until we had gotten married. That's what the rush to the altar was all about.

A month later the marriage was annulled. The experience did little to disabuse me of my romantic notions of marriage, nor did Natalie's divorce from R.J. cause me to give up on the institution. In the years to come it would be said that while Natalie got engaged, I got married. Four more times before I was thirty-five I tried my luck, and four more times I lost. And I'm still a believer.

There is a postscript to Jack Wrather III, and it's a tragic one. Even after all that happened, I have always had a special feeling for him, a mixture of love and sorrow for his deep unhappiness. I heard from him from time to time, but seldom saw him. Then, four years later, my doorbell rang one night. I answered it and there was Jack, smiling one of his most engaging smiles, and my heart almost stopped when I saw it was him. He'd come to say hello and to borrow a pair of cufflinks. He made a great show out of shooting his dangling cuffs out from under his sports jacket. I gave him a pair and a kiss on the cheek when he left. He was married again, with a baby daughter, and he said the marriage was not going well. He committed suicide not long after that.

Natalie stuck close by me through it all, and after the marriage ended I stayed on with her. We were a couple of refugees from relationships gone sour and we banded together to form a mutual support system.

We both dated, but nothing serious. Warren reappeared briefly and disastrously; Jack, too, tried to return but was sent away. Natalie and I decided we had a genius for getting involved with the wrong men. We would prove that theory over and over again in the coming years, and finally Natalie would triumph. It took me a lot longer.

Those were the days of false everything. One night Natalie and I got ready to go out and ended up ruining our mascara with tears of laughter. It had become a sort of ritual, but neither of us had ever realized how absolutely ridiculous it was until this particular night. We began by putting on false eyelashes. Then we would tease and back-comb our hair into bouffants, and then spray the results into a crispy mass of stiff hair. At that time I was spending part of every evening putting on false fingernails, and so when it came time to start piling on the makeup, I had to be particularly careful not to break a nail. Natalie wore falsies. She was stuffing them into her bra when she looked up at me, grinned wickedly, and said, "Did you ever count up all the false things we've got on?"

I hadn't, and so we began an inventory which ended up with us on the floor, helpless from laughter.

"You forgot one," she said finally, still gasping for breath.

"What?" I asked, ready to dissolve into hysterics again.

"Sleeping pills!" We thought this was so funny that it was at least a half-hour before we were even able to look at one another without dissolving in laughter. We both took them, and somehow laughing about it made it more acceptable. What made it slapstick as well is that Natalie had just returned from Europe with the latest in sleeping pills—one that came in the form of a suppository and was faster-acting than regular pills. Natalie was squeamish about inserting the suppository and tended to do it with her eyes closed and her face screwed up in disgust. I would sit on the end of the bed laughing at her. Natalie's bedtime ritual became a private joke which we shared for many years. I was less squeamish, because I knew if I didn't take pills I'd never sleep, and lying awake sorting through the mess my life had become was not a pleasant way to spend the night.

12

I had begun taking sleeping pills—mine were called Placidyl—in the course of a crush I had developed on one of the several men who plotted the course of Natalie's career. He was handsome, powerful, funny, and he responded to me. He was a dose of excitement in a life that lay in the dreary ruins of a bad marriage.

Mornings I was a student at the Hollywood Professional School, determined to complete high school and do reasonably well. I frequently spent nights at Natalie's, but most of the time I lived at home with Mom and Pop. I was determined to finish school and even organized a car pool with several friends to save money and to develop a circle of new friends. One morning we were late, something which never fails to make me nervous. Somebody mentioned it was also Ash Wednesday, and an inspiration hit me. I stuck my finger into the ashtray, rubbed it around, then put a big smudge on my forehead. So did my two girlfriends. We arrived late but with a perfectly acceptable excuse. We'd been to church.

The rest of the day I was one of those pretty young things in tight pants selling clothes at Jax, which was then the place to go in Beverly Hills if you had the figure to get into his clothing. It had its good points and bad points. Good was going in each day and having my pick of the Jax inventory at a considerable discount—Jack Hansen, the owner, liked his help to look good, but because salaries were low and the clothing expensive, he gave us big discounts instead of acceptable salaries. Bad was standing around all day trying to please the unpredictable and not always polite Beverly Hills ladies who came into the shop. It was also something of a challenge to find gracious ways of letting them know they were simply too wide in the beam to get into Jax slim pants. But these ladies were not accustomed to taking no for an answer—in whatever form it came.

At a party with Natalie I met Ed Hookstratten, who was then as now one of the most successful show-business attorneys in Hollywood. He is also a man known for his unshakable loyalties, his good humor, and his ability to bargain hard. Ed was looking for a gal Friday who would be part-time legal secretary and part-time all-around office hand, and I jumped at the chance. I had delusions of competence, and though I could type well enough, I was lost when it came to legalese. Ed was so loyal and thoughtful he probably would have stood by patiently while I learned the profession at his expense. I tried for a while, but then gave up. It didn't seem fair to him or to me. He actually said he was sorry to see me go, and I've remained fond of him ever since.

One of my favorite customers at Jax had been Steve McQueen's wife, Neile, and when I ran into her on the street she asked what I was doing. I replied I was between jobs with no definite plans.

"Why don't you go back to acting? You were good, you know."

I was flattered and astonished. I also felt a bit weak in the knees. I thanked her and then went home to talk to Natalie. I was actually considering returning to something I had literally revolted against several years earlier. In the interim I had failed at marriage and was not exactly optimistic about my future in the working world. Natalie heard me out.

"If it's what you want to do, then do it," she said when I was finished.

Neile beat her to it. She had acted on her own suggestion and had called the producer of *Dr. Kildare*, then a hit series starring Richard Chamberlain, and said I would be perfect for a part they were having trouble casting. I went in for a reading and got the role.

What had once been terrifying and uncomfortable for me was now, if not yet a pleasure, certainly preferable to Jax or being a secretary. I approached acting this time as a job, and I was determined to do my best. I followed Natalie's example and was always prompt—often a bit early—and I always knew my lines. I knew this was especially important in television, which was far more a business than an art form.

Money was king in television and those who delivered the goods were favored over those who were difficult, temperamental, and, as I heard it put most disdainfully, artistic.

Evenings I either spent at home with Natalie or with the man I had become involved with. Because he was one of those who made some of Natalie's professional decisions, he was in a position to help me, too. I did not ask, since it might create a conflict of interest for him, but soon he was seeing to it that my name got around.

We became lovers, and when this happened I let Natalie know. She didn't object, but she didn't enthuse, either.

"Just don't marry him," she said. "He's the wandering kind."

I followed her advice, which was easy to do, since the subject of matrimony never came up. Instead, I got pregnant. We had taken precautions, but there it was, and the day I was told, I went straight home and got violently ill. Natalie just got violent. She telephoned him and ordered him to come to the house at once. When he arrived, she really let him have it. Natalie had a strong moral sense, and when it was violated, she retaliated forcefully. She was also somewhat old-fashioned by the standards of the day, and so was I. I knew marriage would not work with him, but I also knew that I could not be the mother of an illegitimate child. In those days that was a real stigma for the child as well as the mother.

It took a lot of telephone calls, but Natalie finally

found what she considered the most trustworthy abortionist in Tijuana. He happened to be located in a building just a couple of blocks from where I had been married about a year before. Shaking, certain I was risking my life, I went in. The clinic knew I was not one of their ordinary patients—there had been phone calls, a visit from someone Natalie sent to check the place out, and there was a well-dressed man waiting downstairs in his expensive car. The doctor and the nurse kept asking me who I was, and I never told them. Finally, it was done.

Once we were back in Los Angeles, Natalie made her move. She reminded him she had asked him not to date me, not to be my lover, and to leave me alone. She told him I had trouble enough in my life already without this, too. She repeated it all to him once again. And then she fired him.

I asked her to reconsider, but she was adamant. Years later I ran into him and we went and had a drink and spent the entire time apologizing to one another. I told Natalie what had happened, but she said nothing. Natalie was not exactly a forgiving person, though in many instances it was just a matter of time and experience before she could overlook what had once been unacceptable to her.

Natalie and I were dining together a few weeks after I'd had drinks with my former lover. I looked up over coffee and saw him enter the restaurant. I motioned for him to come to our table and saw him hesitate as Natalie looked up and recognized him. He paused, then approached. She invited him to sit down for a drink. We all chatted briefly and then he stood to leave. When he did, Natalie reached up, pulled him down, and gave him a kiss on the cheek. I blinked back my tears.

He is now one of the heads of a major studio and we have worked together professionally, and I think if we ever talked the whole experience over—and I doubt we ever will, though we are cordial whenever we meet—I think we would both wonder what it was we saw in each other in the first place.

I tried Natalie's patience, her love, and her loyalty. I had set out determined to go through life never making a wave, never causing any sort of disruption, especially in Natalie's life. And here I was screwing up all over the place. Natalie had helped me through the last unhappy years at home, out of a lousy marriage, through an abortion, and had never once left my side. I vowed once again to make no trouble and set myself the task of becoming a good actress. I worked diligently, and often.

I also got typecast. I had long since ceased being a skinny little kid who drank Weight-On and felt inferior about my looks. I was five-feet-two and had a good figure, including a chest that seemed to go on forever. I was well aware of my assets and, given the business I was in, knew they worked to my advantage. I was also Natalie Wood's sister, and though the similarities between us were noticeable, the differences were positively striking. Natalie's beauty was soft and sensual, her eyes dark and her manner seductive. I was sensual, but not soft. I have blue eyes, freckles aplenty, and with my figure I come across more sexpot than seductress. I was also outspoken, a bit opinionated, and not at all hesitant when it came to speaking up. I was diplomatic enough, but not one to be easily intimidated. Whenever I was cast in a part, it was invariably as the stacked secretary, the mistress, the tough tootsie, the wisecracking broad, the whore with the heart of tin or sometimes gold. I dreamed of playing a college professor who wore glasses, carried volumes of Shelley around with her, and was in love —unrequited, of course—with the tall, handsome professor who occupied the office next door. It hasn't happened yet.

13

Natalie at work. Everyone who ever came in contact with her considered her to be one of those rare hardworking professionals who keep their temper in check, always know their lines, and take their direction well. There was about her a sense of dedication which, in later years, was supplanted by indomitable willpower. If something did not work of its own accord, she would make it work by the sheer force of her will. She had to. She went on gut instinct, and there was a certain amount of panic when she was occasionally reminded of the fact that the only thing she could depend on was guts. She had no training, no special capabilities—just plenty of guts.

Work was a given in her life, and so was stardom. Since she had been a child there was somebody there to dress her, to do her hair, pick out her wardrobe, put on her makeup, polish her shoes, coach her with her lines, fly her from city to city. She accepted it all, never complained, and lived with the attitude "This is what I do, and these are the things that are due me."

Natalie getting ready for a film was a picture of iron will. As soon as she had a start date for shooting, she followed a strict regimen. She gave up drinking, smoking—that much later—and began to exercise. She was among the most reluctant exercisers but she knew its benefits and kept at it with dogged regularity. I am somewhat more athletic and quite often I would drop by her house and we'd go together to the guest house out behind her pool and exercise, always with the hope that conversation would make the time pass and the sweat come faster. It usually did.

The guest house was that and more. There was a downstairs guest suite and an upstairs guest suite. A spacious ranch-style den was filled with trophies, photographs, and a big-screen television set. There was a Jacuzzi and an exercise room with ballet bar and Universal gym equipment.

She was extremely conscious of her weight—not that she was in any way heavy, but she worried that she might get overweight, and well aware that the camera makes you look heavier, she dieted religiously for every film she ever made. In later years she began taking diet pills, a habit which caused her to have occasional mood swings or to become anxious and irritable, but she paid the price and lost the pounds. She also took diuretics and experimented with natural appetite suppressants. She drank gallons of KB-11 tea, which she insisted was the world's best diuretic, and she ate little clumps of tuna in which it was impossible to find even a trace of mayonnaise. She gained fifty-four pounds when she was pregnant with Courtney, which, as Natalie moaned one day, "was almost a whole other person." Following Courtney's birth Natalie retired to the desert and emerged several months later minus the pounds. Usually there were not many to lose, but because she was small, and her metabolism was slower than most, they were never easy to shed.

Natalie once said she wouldn't be a true Russian if she didn't drink, and drinking certainly figured in our childhood. Hardly a night would go by that Natalie did not have her cocktails or, in later years, wine. But when it came time to work, the drinking stopped. While everyone around her had wine with dinner, she would drink ice water and chew on fresh vegetables. Her refusal to drink while she was working held fast until *Brainstorm*, when she began staying around the set several afternoons a week and drinking with the crew. By the time she made *Brainstorm* there had been several unsuccessful pictures, her career was in jeopardy, and the pressure was obviously such that she dropped her ban on drinking at work.

There were pictures she enjoyed making, others that she disliked. A film crew is a peculiar mixture of people gathered together for the purpose of creating an illusion. When they go on location, a film crew is almost like a microcosm of life: relationships are formed and dissolved, and there is an intimacy few other professions have. It is an intimacy that more often than not is also sexual. You are away from your customary relationships, and new relationships are substituted. You are away from your real family, so another, very temporary family is formed. Natalie, when she was not married, was no exception. Her relationship with Warren Beatty followed her working with him.

Robert Redford, by the time Natalie met him, was well on his way to going from leading man to superstar. But when we first saw him it was quite a different story. He had a small part on *The Eleventh Hour*, and when the show aired, I happened to see him. I thought he was just gorgeous so I telephoned Natalie and told her about him. Natalie got hold of a tape of the show and looked at it.

"Gosh, he's really good-looking," she said afterward. "But what do we do about those bumps on his face? Maybe they're just pimples and he's having a bad week."

"Well, they look like bumps to me."

Several years later Natalie telephoned and resumed the conversation. "They really are bumps," she announced. "I met him. He's gorgeous and he's very nice too."

She adored Robert Redford and would have been more than willing to go out with him but Redford was a married man and one who was widely known for staying close to home. On the set of *Inside Daisy Clover* I went bounding by his portable dressing room onstage—it was right next to Natalie's—and his door came ajar, no doubt because of the uneven flooring on the soundstage. There stood Robert Redford in his boxer shorts, nothing else. I grinned at him, he grinned back and closed the door. I rushed in to tell Natalie, who looked at me and laughed.

"Sometimes I think you have all the luck," she told me.

Her friendship with Redford and his wife, Lola, was an enduring one. When he was making *The Candidate,* he called and asked Natalie to play an unbilled cameo as herself. She agreed, and thereafter, though they did not work together again, they remained good friends and often talked of making another picture together. She knew it was only talk, though, and told the rest of us that Redford's reputation for being indecisive about film projects would prevent another collaboration.

It was her nature, and tended to be the custom among her contemporaries as well, not to discuss sexual or romantic conquests. Where I was concerned she sometimes made exceptions to this rule. Natalie and I both walked a thin line between what we needed and what was acceptable to our background and society. For instance, when she made *Love with the Proper Stranger* with Steve McQueen, she was on the rebound from Warren and, in general, feeling punitive toward him. I saw her and Steve working together and sensed a closeness that went beyond the camera. Later, when I asked, she looked up and grinned wickedly—the closest I think she could come to a leer, which was not very close at all. I hope it happened, because it could have provided her with comfort during some unhappy times.

I do know he unintentionally provided her with a

punch line which she shared only with me—because I was the only one to whom it could possibly mean anything. Some years before Natalie made *Love with the Proper Stranger,* a manufacturer of motor scooters got the idea that if he presented Natalie with a scooter, she'd ride it all over town and make it the rage of Hollywood. The offer was made and Natalie accepted, on the condition the manufacturer provide a scooter for me, too.

"I'm not going out there all alone," she said. "After all, look at all those weird people riding around on motorcycles."

In due course, two bright red motor scooters arrived at Natalie's. A perspiring man patiently explained how to drive them, and Natalie and I took off. We careened down to Sunset Boulevard, screaming all the way, hysterically shouting instructions to each other. We made it nearly to Beverly Hills before losing our nerve and turning back toward home. We were tooling along, none too steadily, when a car cut in front of Natalie and sent her skidding off Sunset. That did it. We abandoned the scooters and walked home. That was the last either of us saw of our red scooters. The incident was filed away in our memories until one day during the shooting of Natalie's movie with Steve. Natalie came upon Steve on the narrow street outside the soundstage. He was tinkering with one of his beloved motorcycles.

"I had one once," she volunteered. And then she told him the whole story. He listened, and when she was done, he looked up at her, not sure he really believed what finally had happened.

"You really left them? Just walked away?"

"Yes."

"Are you shittin' me?"

Ever after, whenever Natalie or I heard a story which inspired the least bit of incredulity, we'd call one another and play through the entire tale just so the other could deliver Steve's punch line.

He was a sweet, uncomplicated man who had a way of getting right to the point, a way of sensing trouble and dealing with it. I was between husbands, between jobs, and depressed. I dropped by the set of *The Reivers* one day, hoping to see an old friend, and Steve walked up and started chatting. We talked for a few minutes, and I noticed he was watching me very carefully. Finally he took me by the hand and walked me to his dressing room, shut the door, and said, with that lopsided grin of his, "Tell me, maybe I can help."

His lecture on the ins and outs of life was enlightening. When I felt vulnerable and used, he urged fighting back and striking out on my own. He stressed the importance of being your own person and not depending upon others as a source of validation and support. It was one of those well-timed pep talks, the sort I'd always expected one got from one's parents, but I got mine from Steve McQueen. In the years to come, whenever I'd see him I'd kiss him on the cheek, and he would always pat my hand. He was the most decent of men, a straightforward person full of street smarts which compensated for his lack of formal education. He gave me his friendship and made no other demands of me, which endeared him to me forever.

Natalie was a devout worker, but she was not above a bit of malingering on occasion—particularly if she was having trouble with her part, her director, or felt otherwise unappreciated. She was in the throes of all three when I visited the *West Side Story* set. She approached the role of Maria with great trepidation, acutely uncomfortable playing a Puerto Rican and unhappy that the songs were to be dubbed in by Marnie Nixon. No sooner had she started shooting than another problem developed: she had trouble responding to her director, Robert Wise, and he to her. She complained privately that he was always more interested in the logistics of the picture than he was in the people who were in it. Natalie particularly needed a director's attention on this picture. She was well aware of her limitations, and equally well aware she was taking a big risk playing this role.

She was also very anxious about the dancing sequences, and on the day I was there they were on a break between setups on one of them. For just about anyone else in the world, sneaking a day off isn't all that difficult. For an actor in the midst of making a picture, it's virtually impossible. A day off can cost a studio thousands of dollars, insurance companies become suspicious, and consequently there are all sorts of conditions for getting off the lot. That day Natalie decided she wanted to go home. And she had a plan.

If she could prove she had a fever, the insurance company would pay off for the day and she could go home. She complained of a fever and went to her dressing room. I followed with a glass of hot water from the coffee cart. An assistant director sent for the doctor, and Natalie and I worked furiously to mush up a bar of soap in hot water. She'd heard somewhere that soap in the hot water retained heat. I ran for another cup of water, and then we rehearsed what we would do.

Natalie would be lying on the settee in her dressing room when the doctor arrived. While he took her temperature I was to begin exclaiming over pain in my "trick" knee and to ask the doctor to examine it. This was to be accomplished with his back toward Natalie, who would be busy plunging the thermometer into the bar of soap. I think that by the time the doctor arrived I had a fever from anticipation, but we went ahead with our charade and it worked perfectly.

Except for one thing. The bar of soap didn't change the temperature a bit, and despite our elaborate planning, Natalie finished up at 98.8 and was certified well enough to work. She did two more set-ups that afternoon and then left, one of the few times I've ever seen her walk away from her work. She went home, took a long bath, had a long session with her analyst, and was back at work the next morning.

Natalie had a sense of humor, but she did not like jokes. During the making of *The Great Race*, jokes were the order of the day. Strike one. It was also a long and difficult picture to make, requiring great stretches on location. Strike two. It was a film full of men who created their own sense of camaraderie. Strike three. That sense of camaraderie centered primarily around the director, Blake Edwards, a man she was not thrilled with. Strike four. That's one strike too many even in the American League, and whenever she was asked if she'd ever made a picture which was decidedly not a pleasure, she would cite *The Great Race*, but was always careful not to be too specific.

The company was on location in Lone Pine, California, one of the more uninteresting spots of the world, for what seemed like forever. Natalie called and insisted I come up for a visit, and she even included Carl Brent, who was then my husband, in her invitation. That proved she was desperate, at least to me, because Natalie had been very open in her disapproval of my marrying for the second time. I was eighteen, though, and felt I could make it work. Also, I still fit easily into Natalie's life. It was, after all, the only one I really knew. So off we went.

The day we arrived, Natalie's stunt double broke her wrist. The next day, Carl, who had brought his motorcycle to give him something to do, went riding off into the hills. Natalie and I sat under an umbrella out of the sun and talked, and then she'd go off and do a scene. Finally we noticed that the sun was disappearing and Carl had not returned. Natalie sent a teamster to look for him and before long the teamster came back with what was left of Carl's motorcycle and what was left of Carl. There was much more of the latter than the former. Carl had a broken collarbone and was in considerable pain.

Natalie went into high gear. She had us all driven to a tiny airport with a dirt runway, found a pilot and a plane and rented both, then we all helped load Carl into the plane. Natalie and I scrambled into the backseat. Just as the plane was taking off, the door immediately beside Carl, who was in the copilot's seat, swung open. Natalie and I started screaming and holding on to Carl, who, of course, hadn't fastened his seat belt. He couldn't and it hadn't occurred to any of us to do it for him.

We finally got Carl to a hospital, and while the doctors worked on him, Natalie and I sat in a waiting room drinking coffee. She kept saying she didn't know what else possibly could go wrong on the picture, but she was certain something would. She was dreading the pie-fight scene. It was not easy, she kept saying, to look pretty with pie on your face.

Natalie finally went off to the bathroom to clean up, and while I waited I pulled her script out of the shoulder bag she had carried with her on the plane. I was casually thumbing through it, looking over the notes she always made in the margin, when I saw something which stunned me.

In the margin next to a chunk of her dialogue, a speech that was to be very direct and pointed, Natalie had written, "Say this like Lana would."

I was thrilled; there were tears streaming down my cheeks when Natalie walked back into the room.

"What's the matter?" she asked, obviously thinking the day's events were too much for me.

"I'm happy," I cried.

"Here?" she said, nodding in the direction of the hospital emergency room. "Now?" she added, looking at me in utter confusion.

"Yes," I said. And I never told her why.

14

When the marriage to R.J. was over and the romance
with Warren had ended—and a second marriage and
a family were still in the future—Natalie occasionally
relaxed and sometimes even enjoyed herself. One
summer she rented a house in Malibu and I moved in
with her. We were on the beach by day, Natalie getting a gorgeous tan and me getting tan in between
my freckles. At the time neither of us was involved
with a man on a steady basis, and so we played the
field. One of the field was a funny young comedian
named Sam Thomas, who was in between jobs and
recovering from an unsuccessful romance. Sam was
wonderful company and we both adored him.

I had been dating a man who had taught me to play
darts, except that instead of real darts we used a gun
with rubber-tipped darts. I had my dart gun with me
one day while Sam, Natalie, and I sunbathed. I was
feeling mischievous and so I began shooting darts at
Sam. He finally wrestled my gun away from me.

Getting the gun back from Sam became a major
issue early that evening, and by the time the sun was

setting on the horizon—and sunset on the ocean is late during the height of summer solstice—we had consumed a bottle of wine, I had my dart gun back (on sworn promise not to shoot at Sam anymore), and the three of us were walking along the beach, laughing and having a grand time. As we walked, I began tossing rocks into the water, and so I handed my dart gun to Sam, who put it in his pocket.

A good bit down the beach from Natalie's house was a restaurant-bar that was famous for its private little dining rooms looking out on the ocean, rooms equipped with sofas. There were said to be both women and men available as companions. It was strictly Sin City, and its reputation was known to us all, and there were always jokes being made about the place.

"I wonder how business is at that joint," Natalie said as we walked by.

"Depends on what business you're talking about," Sam answered.

"Let's go in and have a drink," Natalie suggested. We had walked a good distance by then and we were all thirsty. The only way to get into the restaurant was through the back door—a wall blocked us from the front entrance along Pacific Coast Highway. We knocked on the door several times, and finally Natalie pounded her fist against it. The bartender opened it and saw three sandy and disheveled people, refused to let us enter through that door, and insisted we come in the front way. That, we explained, was impossible because the wall blocked our way. He was gruff and unmovable.

"Shoot him, Sam!" Natalie yelled.

"Shoot him! Shoot him!" I immediately chimed in.

Sam pulled my dart gun out of his pocket and pointed it at the stunned man. In the dark it looked like the real thing.

"Hand over your money," Natalie ordered.

"Yeah. All of it," I added. Natalie looked positively menacing. I imagined I looked like somebody about to burst into hysterical laughter. Sam appeared as dangerous as he could, which wasn't very dangerous at all.

The bartender was appropriately terrified, and I noticed that his hand, which was resting on the door-knob, started shaking.

"Shit," he said. And then he slammed the door in our faces. We ran off as fast as we could. Later, back in Natalie's house, trying to catch our breath, Natalie was seized by still another inspiration.

"Sam, do as I say," she ordered. After a careful rehearsal, Sam telephoned the restaurant, and posing as a Malibu sheriff, told the restaurant that two young women and a young man had committed armed robbery in Malibu canyon and had been spotted less than an hour ago near the restaurant. It must have been the bartender himself, because he bit.

"They just tried to hold us up," he yelled into the phone. Natalie and I had our hands over our mouths to stifle our screams.

"Then listen carefully. They are dangerous. Get

everybody away from the windows. Better still, clear everybody out of the restaurant. They'll probably be back. We'll have a patrol car there in a few minutes."

Sam hung up and the three of us jumped into Natalie's car and raced for the restaurant. We stopped short of the place and saw the parking lot full of people, most of them still holding their drinks. The bartender was standing there in his apron. He still didn't recognize Natalie Wood.

Natalie and I always looked back on this as one of the daring escapades of our single days. We were co-conspirators again when I began dating a very wealthy man named Fletcher Jones, who had his own airplane and a big ranch near Santa Barbara, not to mention just about everything else a man could want —including lots of women. He became interested in me, and soon we were dating steadily. He was older, very handsome, very powerful, and before long I was crazy about him.

Natalie was dating an attractive young agent, David Andrews, who spoke with a Southern drawl. When Fletcher insisted we all fly up to his ranch for dinner, Natalie invited David as her date. It was all very lavish, complete with Fletcher's elegant Polish butler. What formality there was I destroyed by telling a Polish joke, and then, realizing my gaffe, I proceeded to fall all over myself apologizing profusely. I was so embarrassed I was stuttering. Finally I managed to politely tell the butler that he had my permission to tell the nastiest Russian joke he knew. At that moment he looked down at me and moved ahead by several points.

"I couldn't possibly do that," he replied evenly. "They are all far too long." Natalie had to leave the table and go to the bathroom, she was laughing so hard.

Several weeks later Fletcher and I were going to dinner when he called and, sounding like the voice of doom, said his friend Mary Ann Mobley had just been told she had breast cancer and he was going to spend the evening with her. I not only understood, I was so upset for Mary Ann that I telephoned Natalie and told her, and she too became upset for Mary Ann.

I was curled up on my bed that night at about eleven-thirty when Natalie telephoned. She was at a party, and Fletcher was there with Mary Ann. Natalie had made an oblique inquiry and had discovered that Mary Ann had been dating Fletcher off and on for some time and that she most definitely did not have breast cancer.

"Her boobs are fine, and bursting out of her dress right now," Natalie hissed.

Fletcher called the next day, brimming with contrition, figuring quite correctly Natalie had given me a full report. I refused his invitation to dinner that night, refused the flowers that arrived a few hours later, and refused the bracelet from Tiffany's that arrived a few hours after that. I spent the next several days sending back Fletcher's gifts.

Natalie told me she and David Andrews were casual friends and that there was nothing romantic in their relationship. He was often around, he was charming, and he had a sense of humor. When he asked me out on a date, I didn't even bother to ask Natalie if it was okay with her. I figured it was, and frankly, I was interested in him. By our third date, we became lovers.

We remained lovers for a while until the afternoon Natalie called and invited me to dinner.

"I can't, I've got a date with David," I said.

"You've got what?"

I explained.

"I'll be right over," Natalie said. Fifteen minutes later she was sitting on the edge of my bed, confessing that she, too, was having an affair with David Andrews, but that she hadn't said anything about it to anyone because it wasn't serious and, she admitted, she felt embarrassed about it. Besides, she never figured David would go after me, too.

It seems odd in retrospect, but it didn't occur to either of us to get mad or to be hurt. What we wanted was to get even. We hatched a plan. I called David first, and told him I couldn't wait to see him that evening. I said I was depressed, lonely, and would be waiting for him at seven-thirty. Natalie telephoned him next, and she, too, said she was lonely and depressed and absolutely had to see him. At eight P.M. He hemmed, hawed, pleaded the press of business, but Natalie was not to be dissuaded.

My phone rang less than an hour later, and Natalie and I sat there and let it ring. We knew it was David, and figured he was calling me to beg off for the evening. We let him sweat it out.

He was due to arrive at my apartment first, and at seven-thirty he showed up, a bunch of flowers in his hand, and when he saw Natalie and me all dressed up and waiting for him, all of the color drained from his face.

"Well, David"—Natalie smiled sweetly—"time to make a choice. Which one of us will it be?"

We let him swing in the wind, and we enjoyed every minute of his agony, almost as much, Natalie said later, as we had enjoyed our time in bed with him. David just stood there speechless, trying to find some way to extricate himself from this mess. He was still sputtering, trying to say something, when Natalie spoke again.

"Good-bye, David," she said, and with that she stood up and opened the door. David left.

Over dinner that night at Chasen's, Natalie winked at me and said, "That will teach him to mess with the Wood sisters."

15

The moments of silliness and play—which were rare at best—grew more infrequent as Natalie bore down on her psychoanalysis and her career, two goals which were sometimes at war with one another. She was reluctant to leave her analyst for long locations and passed up a number of pictures in order to deal with her private demons in therapy.

Whatever her personal unhappiness, the image she presented to the world was that of Natalie Wood, Movie Star. She was always turned out, even when she wasn't turned on by what she was doing. She was conscious of her image to such an extent that when I asked her one day if she even wore makeup to her daily sessions with her analyst she looked at me as if I were daft.

"Of course," she said. I don't think it ever occurred to her to do otherwise.

She was groomed and jeweled for every occasion. She had every Judith Leiber belt ever designed, handbags in every skin imaginable and in every color, and a wardrobe that literally filled rooms. I once arrived at her house for a big party wearing a silk blouse I had just splurged on. Natalie spotted it the minute I came in, asked me where I got it, and quickly turned to her secretary and said, "Get me one." Almost as an afterthought she asked me what colors they came in. I remembered five. Natalie ordered four.

Nothing, however, compared to her jewelry collection. She had a knack for combining small pieces of jewelry, bracelets or necklaces, linking them together with stunning results. One of her favorites was an antique Russian medallion, shaped something like a fleur-de-lis, made out of dark blue cloisonné, which she wore around her neck. It had been a gift from R.J. When she went to Russia to make a TV special (she loathed Russia), she brought back a string of Fabergé eggs in the form of a necklace, probably worth a small fortune (and on Natalie it looked worth much more than that).

She was meticulous about caring for her jewelry, and I recall only one occasion when a good piece was sent hurtling into oblivion. Mom and I were on hand consoling her just after the breakup of her marriage to Richard Gregson. The three of us were in the dressing room adjoining Natalie's bedroom. Natalie, her head in her hands, was swearing revenge on Richard. Mom and I were counseling moderation. Suddenly Natalie looked up, whipped open her jewelry box, and pulled out the elegant wedding ring Richard had bought her. It was a lovely, intricate band laced with blue sapphires, designed by Buccellati. She threw the ring into the wastebasket. Mom dived for the wastebasket and retrieved the ring.

"If you're throwing it away, can I have it?"

"Do whatever you want with it. I never want to see it again."

Mom wore that ring—but never in Natalie's presence—for several years, until it was stolen in a robbery at her apartment. She is presently wearing a former wedding ring of mine, a diamond band which, when the marriage blew up, I presented to her. The passion Natalie and I shared for jewelry did not begin with us.

Natalie also possessed the World's Largest Collection of Sunglasses. It is not an understatement to say that Natalie was a sunglasses freak. She would spot a rack of them in a store, begin her inspection, then make her choices, which were always plural, never singular. In the hall just outside her bedroom was a side table under a five-foot-nine mirror. On the table was a very large silver tray, and on the tray, row after row, were Natalie's sunglasses. She would emerge from her bedroom made-up and dressed to kill, then pause and begin the ritual of selecting a pair of sunglasses to go with her outfit. She never proceeded down the stairs until she was certain she'd selected exactly the right pair. It didn't matter how long it took or who was waiting.

Natalie maintained strict control over the image she presented to the world. Tommy Thompson was her unofficial press secretary. He moved to California when *Life* magazine folded, and he and Natalie became even closer friends. Tommy went on to become a very successful best-selling author, but whenever it was time for Natalie to launch a few public comments to the press, it was usually Tommy who did the writing. In Hollywood, your power increases in proportion to your fame and success, and so does your ability to control what is written about you. A very few—Barbra Streisand, Robert Redford, Goldie Hawn are among them—ask for and usually receive what is called "quote approval." That means they see and edit every word supposedly uttered by them before it sees print. They also often have photo approval. Natalie had both quote and photo approval, and because it was usually Tommy doing the writing, she also had text approval. They were collaborators as well as close friends.

Mom picked up a copy of *Cosmo* one day and read a story by Tommy about Natalie, and immediately called me.

"How could he?" she cried. "He was her friend! And then he goes and talks about the pills and things."

The article had been about how happy Natalie and R.J. were now that they were back together and had a child of their own. It also talked about Natalie's abandoning her habit of sleeping pills and of some of the unhappier moments of her life. The overall impression of the article was that here was a ravishingly beautiful lady who had gone through some rough times but was now back on top of the world. It was exactly as Natalie intended it, she had seen every word of it, and it was also pretty much the truth.

In fact, she'd had a purpose in planting the article. Natalie wasn't working a whole lot, and she wanted to make it known that she was available, together, and absolutely smashing. She was—on the advice of the press agent she employed at the time—burnishing her image a bit. Nothing unusual about that by Hollywood standards, it's done all the time.

Natalie's control over what was written about her did not extend to critics, and she suffered their slings and arrows with good sportsmanship and carefully hid the fact that every negative comment hurt. When she was given Harvard's Lampoon Award as the worst actress of the year for about the fourth time, Natalie and her press agent came up with an absolutely inspired response. Natalie offered to go to Harvard to collect the award in person. She did exactly that, only to be kidnapped by a group of students who had in mind a publicity stunt of their own. There were several frightening moments, but she was finally freed and went up onstage to accept the award and to express her thanks. It was Natalie's firm —and absolutely correct—belief that if she could spend some time with her enemies, they would be enemies no more. She could win over the Harvard student body just as easily as she could win over a critic. The problem was that critics—with a few exceptions, most of them in Los Angeles—were not given to consorting with movie stars. No matter. Natalie could charm her enemies and create friendships out of animosity.

Natalie's control over the press collapsed about the time her career went into decline. Before that, her power was absolute. At one point, when she wasn't married and didn't especially wish to talk about her life and career, *Ladies' Home Journal* asked to do a story on her. Through her press agent, Natalie communicated her customary demands: quote and photo approval. *Ladies' Home Journal* responded by offering photo approval, but refused quote approval. A brief negotiation took place, and it ended with the *Journal* dropping the project. A short time later, word reached Natalie that the magazine had decided to do a story by going around to all of her friends and asking questions about her. Natalie's response was a few carefully chosen telephone calls. A wall of silence descended upon the *Journal*'s reporter, and the story was never done.

16

In the early spring of 1964, shortly after my eighteenth birthday, Carl Brent and I were married in Las Vegas. He chose Las Vegas because he loved to gamble and I went along with it because I was enchanted by the notion that I was loved.

Carl had been insistent about our marriage and I had been at first reluctant. Finally I weighed the pros and cons, and though the list was virtually even, I agreed. It seemed to me that all my life I had been looking for security—emotional or financial—and Carl held out the possibility of both. He was both accepting and forgiving about my abortion. He was also a member of that circle of the semiglamorous to which I wanted to belong. I confessed to Carl that I wasn't really in love. "In like" would be more the case. He insisted I could love him in time.

Natalie was, once again, less than pleased by the idea, but when I said I was going through with it, she accepted the inevitable and sent me off with a hug. There was no honeymoon, because Carl had work to do and I was excited about furnishing my first apartment.

I went about buying furniture for the small apartment we had rented in the Barrington Plaza just off Sunset Boulevard, one of those showbiz high-rises full of New York actors and other colorful people. Carl was very busy. He was preparing to travel as Judy Garland's road manager on a tour of Australia, a gigantic logistical exercise complicated by the demands of the star herself.

I met Judy immediately after our marriage. She was then married to a man named Mark Herron, who was allegedly her manager, but it seemed to me as I came to know them that Judy made all the decisions, and not always well. Judy was gracious and witty— and sober some of the time (most of the time she was not). All the things I'd heard about her, that she was pathologically insecure, unstable, and one of the most delightful people you'd ever want to know, were absolutely true.

When we took off for Australia, I was the only woman besides Judy in our group of, as I remember it, six. Judy traveled with Mark, her conductor, her agent, her publicist, and Carl. She settled down in her seat, ordered a drink, and kept right on drinking. Hours later—the transpacific flight is a long one, even in a jet—when we had left Honolulu on the long, long leg to Sydney, Judy went off to the bathroom to put on a robe and sleep awhile. She was too drunk to change her clothes and so I helped her, and from then on my function on the Down Under Tour was defined. I helped Judy in and out of her clothes when she couldn't manage by herself, which was quite a lot of the time. My other job was to intercept all cleaning and other deliveries and inspect them for pins or any other sharp objects with which she might hurt herself. It was a major responsibility, and though Carl helped me when he could, I was pretty much left to handle Judy alone.

Backstage before each concert she was a mass of exposed nerves, convinced the audience was going to hate her. It was a fear she'd lived with all of her incredible career. Now that she was near the end and sensed it, fear turned to panic. The Australian concerts were not her best. Nobody told Judy, of course, and such suggestions as were made were submitted most carefully. I, on the other hand, had never seen her perform and was captured by her magic and was open in my admiration of her.

There were occasional rest stops on the tour, but not for Carl. He always had to set up the next performance, work that was complicated and time-consuming, all the more so because Judy was quick to spot mistakes and complain about them. When he had a few hours off, Carl would magically find a card or dice game and a group of men to gamble with him. I found his interest in gambling a minor irritant. When one of the men on the tour teased him about his losses, I began to worry. I asked about it, and he smiled, kissed me, and said, "Everything's fine. Don't worry."

Carl was a first-rate stage manager, and his work

on Judy's tour—which was a triumph for her, too, despite the misgivings of her entourage—secured his reputation. Nevertheless, even successful stage managers have sometimes long lulls of unemployment between even longer tours. Carl began to wait for another tour, and I waited with him.

Back in Los Angeles we saw Judy and Mark frequently at first, then less often as everybody got busy with other projects. Carl and I spent a lot of time at Judy's house, adults gathered in one room, Lorna and Joey Luft in another, running the films Judy kept around for the kids. I spent a while with the adults; then, when nobody noticed, I slipped off and watched movies with the kids. Judy was less a legend to me now than a deeply troubled lady and I was often uncomfortable around her. One of the films I watched with Judy's children was *Francis, the Talking Mule*, and I loved it. As I look back now, it is obvious to me that I was still a child myself, living in a make-believe world and not at all prepared for life as an adult.

I decided it would help if I went back to work. I began making the rounds of auditions and readings, and grabbed the occasional part. I bounded out of bed every morning ready to tackle the world; Carl stayed home and tried to hide his unhappiness. He insisted his gambling debts were small and his losses were minimal. I did not then and do not now have any sense of money. I was never taught to manage it and even now I do not have a credit card to my name. It's not my way of keeping control of that side of my life. I should have applied the same rule to Carl, but applying my rules to the men in my life was not how I did things.

The situation with Carl deteriorated steadily. I bought two basset hounds to keep him company, but ended up taking care of them myself, since he was never home.

Late one afternoon I returned from work to find he'd left the dogs locked all day in the hall. I got down on the floor and scrubbed up the dog crap and started crying. Finally it was obvious this marriage had nowhere to go.

I took the puppies and went to Natalie's for the night. There were no tears this time, and Natalie supported every move I made. The next morning I had the locks on the door changed. That afternoon I went to a lawyer. My second marriage had lasted all of six months.

Carl offered little protest. It was as obvious to him as it was to me that the marriage had been a mistake. The last I heard of him—years ago—was that he'd left show business and gone home to Mississippi and started a business.

I kept the apartment and plunged into work with a vengeance. This time I had good luck. I was put under contract at Twentieth Century-Fox—Natalie's old stomping ground—to the delight of both my sister and my mother. I was cast in the television-series version of *The Long, Hot Summer,* playing the part Lee Remick had done so well in the film version. It was the usual simmering sexpot role, nothing new to me.

But being in a series was, and the idea of it caused me no small amount of anxiety.

To make matters worse, the cast of the series changed constantly. I auditioned with Tom Skerritt, who had already been cast for the pilot. We shot the pilot and Tom vanished. By the time we were ready to shoot the first show of the series—we had been picked up for thirteen episodes—everyone in the cast except Edmond O'Brien and me had been replaced, sometimes twice. I came to work every day expecting the ax to fall. Tom Stern came in at one point to play Ben Quick, that richly Faulknerian character, and one day he wasn't there and Roy Thinnes was in his place. Worse, the shifting around of actors continued even after the series started to air. In the first thirteen episodes there were no less than three different Jody Varners.

I was on the rebound from a marriage gone wrong and feeling emotionally vulnerable, both personally and professionally, and so I ended up doing what too many actresses do: I fell in love with a tall, witty director. He was from the Los Angeles theater community, full of restless creative energy and talent, and as do many good directors, he had a deep curiosity about actors. He was also married. It quickly became an affair ruled by the quirks of passion, and he was one of the more passionate men I have known. He was not one to wait once the spell was upon him. We had lunches, we went shopping. I wanted a tambourine, he bought me one.

He lived close by and telephoned one day to say

he'd be over in a matter of minutes. He was, and in a matter of minutes his passion was spent.

"Got any aspirin?" he asked as he dressed.

"You have a headache?"

"No, no. I said I was going out to get a bottle of aspirin. I need a bottle of aspirin to take home."

He was leaving, his bottle of aspirin in his hand, when I kissed him and asked, "What do you need for the next time? Mouthwash?" We collapsed from laughter, struck by the sheer absurdity of what we were doing. Not long after that I came to my senses and so did he. Whenever I see him we grin at one another before we embrace.

Natalie and I talked nearly every day while I was making *The Long, Hot Summer*. She had just finished *Gypsy* and was about to begin *Love with the Proper Stranger*, the film for which she'd receive her third Oscar nomination. She was as secure as I was edgy. Love, and a place in the community in which I felt secure, eluded me.

Near the end of shooting *Gypsy* I dropped by the set, and it also happened to be the same day Mom dropped in. Natalie had called to say Mom was coming and we both wanted to be there for the moment when Mom met Rosalind Russell, who was playing the quintessential stage mother. Rosalind, who was about as friendly and gracious as it was possible for a human being to be, charmed Mom, and Mom turned it on for Roz. Natalie and I were fascinated, and we agreed afterward that it probably never occurred to either of them why we wanted them to meet.

"If mama gets married," Natalie sang softly to herself. It was the song Gypsy sang with her sister, wishing their mother would get married—and stay married—just for once.

"No, 'Lana gets married and married,'" I corrected her.

She turned and looked directly at me. "Do you need love that much?"

"Yes."

"Why, Lana?"

"I've never really had any."

"I hope you find it," she said. Then, after a brief pause and without looking up at me, she added, "It isn't easy."

That day I complained about *Long, Hot Summer* and my problems with the scripts, and Natalie sent me out to my car to get the current script. Then we went to work.

Natalie had no formal training as an actress, and it never occurred to her to seek any until near the end of her life. What she did have, by this time, was considerable experience and an ability to work on a gut instinct which seldom failed her. We sat in her dressing room and I read my lines to her.

"How do you feel? What do you feel right there? What do you want to accomplish? What kind of impression are you trying to make?" she asked as I read to her.

I responded whenever I could. She would either

agree or suggest some additional motivation or feeling to express. When she disagreed, she spoke with great care and diplomacy. She did not work on details. She once said she had spent so many years going from film to film, from character to character, that she had never been able to work on the details of her roles. She looked forward to the day when there would be time for delving deep into her characters.

The next morning on the set at Fox I was confident and prepared, and I stayed that way for all thirteen weeks. *The Long, Hot Summer* was just that. It expired from low ratings and a mixed critical reaction. I got a weekly paycheck even after it ended because I was under contract. There was talk of turning *Peyton Place* into a series, and I hoped to be part of it.

17

The breakup of my marriage with Carl, the cancellation of *Long, Hot Summer,* and God knows what else contributed to what I did next. I know for certain only one thing: I was an emotional shambles and I was desperately in need of someone to love me, to approve of me. Such a man came along. He was a professional man who was also socially prominent. He convinced me he loved me, and because of that overwhelming need in me to be convinced of just that, I moved in with him within weeks of our meeting. The plan was to get married soon.

He took an instant dislike to my friends and would not let me invite them to visit. He became verbally abusive and flew into a rage at any real or imagined offense. Then, one night, he appeared in our bedroom in women's underwear and wearing one of my short nighties. I feel sorry for the man and I make no judgment. It was simply something unacceptable to me. I hid my shame and tried to resume my life, such as it was.

I split. Natalie, who had shared my belief that I was

138

making a wise move for once, shook her head in disbelief. I asked to use her guest room for a few weeks, until I got things sorted out.

"Please. I'll only need it for a short time."

Natalie inspected her elegantly manicured fingernails, and without looking at me, had this to say:

"No, that won't be possible right now. Look, Lana, why don't you go get a job as a stewardess? The pay's good and you'll get to see the world."

I stumbled out of her house in tears. Not only would she not let me use her guest room, she wanted to get me on the first plane out of town. I was an embarrassment.

Arguing with Natalie—if arguing's the word—was nearly impossible. She had what I came to think of as her Queen Victoria attitude: if you gave the slightest offense, Natalie made it clear she was not amused. There were no accusations, no verbal assaults, no sharp remarks, just a withering look and a back turned in your face. The only time I remember Natalie shouting full force was at Mom during the Dating Wars. After that, you crossed Natalie at your peril. In later years her invincibility seemed, at least to me, even greater because by that time she was armed with all the verbal paraphernalia of psychoanalysis. Try to discuss anything she might want to avoid and there you had to contend with "I have no problem with that. That's your problem." Natalie knew the slogans of psychological warfare better than anyone else I've

ever known. In my early years, I was absolutely no
match for her. Later, I stopped trying. Natalie, after a
few cool months, warmed to me once more. I was
terrified of offending her again.

18

Natalie soon made the same mistake I had—she fell in love with a director, an intense, serious man who was married and several years her senior. He was charming and gracious, and Natalie was without a man and spending a lot of time alone.

He came along at a particularly desolate time in her life, and precipitated what Natalie in later years referred to as her "slide," though neither Natalie nor any of the few others who knew what was at the bottom of that slide ever mentioned it again.

She was conscience-stricken over her affair. To his credit, he made it clear that he was not about to leave his wife, but Natalie for a time believed she could prevail. I knew nothing about it until the affair was nearing its end. Natalie and I were upstairs in her bedroom, primping for a party, communing at her dressing table, picking our way through what must have amounted to a small fortune in makeup. Suddenly she began weeping.

"I'm having an affair," she cried, "and I'm miserable."

I had somewhat more experience at this sort of thing and immediately guessed what was the matter. "He's married, right?"

"Right. He's married." She told me who he was, how they'd met and how they hoped one day to work together.

For Natalie, the family was inviolate. Now she was the scarlet woman. This worried her greatly.

"I've got to end it," she cried. "I've just got to. But I don't want to. I . . . I . . . I . . ." And she fell into my arms weeping. I did the only thing I could do: I comforted her and promised to support whatever decision she made. I told her all about my director, and when I came to the story about his dashing out for aspirin and his speedy lovemaking, she looked up and laughed.

"He isn't that way at all," she said finally. I helped her repair her ruined eye makeup, and together we went off to the party, where—why is it that lovers are always tormented by such things?—both Natalie's lover and his wife were among the guests. I stuck close to Natalie, but I needn't have bothered. When we left I had a bruise on my arm where Natalie had held on to me.

Natalie let the affair continue a while longer, and then she ended it. She was in tears for several days and depressed for weeks thereafter, but she felt she'd done the right thing. It was a very bad time. She hated endings of any sort, and this one came at a time when she was lonely, unhappy, and trying—without much success—to make a satisfactory life as a single woman.

The only other man in her life was Mart Crowley, her onetime secretary and friend, who was living in the little guest house by her pool, using his spare time to write the play that would become *The Boys in the Band*, and the rest of his time to cheer Natalie up. She, in turn, decided the best cure was work.

She had read a script called *Penelope* and liked it, though her agents argued that it had problems and the prognosis for the movie was not good. It was a comedy about a girl who masters various disguises and robs the bank owned by her husband, a part played by Ian Bannen. Natalie persisted, and her agents resisted. Natalie won. She made *Penelope*. It cured her depression, but *Penelope*, released in 1966, was a critical and financial disaster at a time when Hollywood was in such a state of flux that even an established star like Natalie could not afford a bomb. She took to her bed when the reviews came out, and the only people to see her with any regularity were Mart and her analyst, John Lindon. I popped in and out, and tried to relay upbeat reports to Mom. Natalie wasn't seeing a lot of Mom these days.

I tried to lure her out, but not even the notion of dinner at La Scala, something which usually evoked an immediate acceptance from her, could get her moving. I did the next best thing. I convinced Jean Leon the reputation of his fine restaurant wouldn't be harmed a bit if he prepared just one Italian dinner to go. He agreed and Natalie was charmed by the gesture.

I was so hopeful that Natalie would get better that I must have convinced myself that she had. I don't think I was the only one. Even Mart, who was in closer contact with her than any of her family, seemed to agree. We were wrong.

The call came from Mom. She could hardly talk. I was to take some of my sloppiest clothes, put them in an overnight bag, and go to Cedars of Lebanon Hospital in Hollywood. Natalie had tried to commit suicide and no one was to know. Mart had found her unconscious and taken her to Cedars. She was registered under a pseudonym I've since forgotten except that the first name was Helen. I was to take the clothes to the hospital so that she could leave without being noticed. I asked Mom if she wanted to go to the hospital with me.

"I think it better I stay home," she said. I learned later that Natalie, after she regained consciousness, had insisted Mom not come to Cedars, a wise decision considering Mom's terror of hospitals and her inability to deal with crises involving Natalie.

I stuffed the clothes into a bag, drove to Cedars, and asked for the assumed name. I waited briefly and then an orderly appeared and escorted me through a maze of corridors and finally into a wing of the hospital I never knew existed, which I suppose is exactly as they intended it. I was shown to a chair in the hall outside Natalie's room and told to wait. I was shaking, I was afraid I was going to be sick, and I was desperately worried about Natalie. Within minutes I could hear her voice. She was shouting, but I couldn't tell what she was saying. Her voice was muffled by the door between us. Then I could hear a man shouting back, and when I heard his voice I suddenly knew that the one man who could take care of Natalie was with her. John Lindon was there to fight for Natalie's life, even when she wasn't willing to herself. I felt enormous gratitude.

After nearly an hour, John Lindon came out of the room and sat down next to me. She had swallowed a bottle of sleeping pills, he said, but she was going to be okay. Her stomach had been pumped and he was going to keep her in the hospital overnight just to be sure. He opened the door and let me into her room.

I started crying when I saw her. Her hair was hanging into her face, she was wearing a loose hospital gown, and her face was puffy, her tiny body swollen. I kissed her, then took her hand.

"I didn't want to live anymore," she whispered, looking away.

I reached across, took her chin, and turned her face so that she was looking directly into mine.

"And now you do?"

She looked away again. I sat silently beside her for quite some time, until she looked up and spoke again.

"Now I do."

Before I left she asked if I'd come back and get her in the morning and take her home. I was there at nine-thirty and she was waiting, dressed in my

grungiest clothes—it hadn't ever occurred to me that
Natalie didn't even own anything remotely grungy—
and I drove her home. Mart was there waiting. We
took her to her room, settled her in bed, and she had
only one question.

"Did anyone find out?"

I didn't know, and so I looked to Mart for an answer.

"No one. John Lindon took care of it all. No one
will ever know."

After Natalie drifted off to sleep, I went downstairs
and asked Mart what had happened.

"Warren was here," he said, barely controlling his
fury.

"But what could have happened?"

"All I know is this. Warren came by and they were
talking. Then I heard raised voices and Warren left. I
haven't any idea what they were talking about. When
Warren left, Natalie went upstairs to her bedroom.
That's when she took the pills. Just before she lost
consciousness she must have had second thoughts,
because she started downstairs. I heard her call. I
found her slumped on the stairs."

"Oh, my God. Why?"

Mart had a few choice expletives for Warren
Beatty, whom he'd never much liked, but even Mart
had to agree that it couldn't have been just Warren. It
was an accumulation of misery and worry. Warren's
ill-timed visit was just a part of the problem.

Mom and Pop simply couldn't believe it had happened, and their relief over Natalie's recovery was so

great that they never pressed for answers to the questions they, too, must have had.

With one exception, Natalie's attempted suicide was never mentioned again, not by any one of us. The exception came one day several years later. Natalie and I were sitting by her pool, watching our young daughters play together. I happened to look up and see Natalie's expression, and it was one of great contentment.

"What if you'd known you would one day have all of this?"

"I would have been willing to wait," she answered immediately, looking at me and smiling. "I would have waited forever."

19

I played Sandy Webber on *Peyton Place* for two years. She was from the wrong side of the tracks, a waitress in a waterfront café married to a bullying garage mechanic. She was also given to chasing after Rodney Harrington, who was played by Ryan O'Neal. It would become a case of life imitating television, except that the chase was reversed.

I was making more money than I'd ever made before—and not a minute too soon. I was beginning to believe I was no better at choosing men than I was at managing money. I had had a manager who had given me an allowance and had been taking care of my bills, and one day I telephoned him to ask why I had received a letter from the IRS saying my taxes were delinquent—and *his* phone had been disconnected. Manager and money had vanished and I was one of several actors who were left without so much as a checking account. I was much more careful when I began making money on *Peyton Place*.

We were an instant hit and became an instant—if sometimes battling—family. From 1965 until I left the show in 1967 I was a part of that family and I loved every minute of it. We were a disparate group of people. There was Mia Farrow, who was painfully thin and who ate spinach and cottage cheese every day for lunch. There was Ryan, as handsome as they come, with a wicked sense of humor and a desire to bed as many of us as he could. Barbara Parkins could be friendly or haughty, depending on how the mood struck her, and moods struck her often. Ed Nelson and Tim O'Connor were also jokesters of the first order who could be depended upon to disrupt shooting whenever possible. Ruth Warrick, the matriarch of the series—and presently the matriarch on the soap *All My Children*—was also the matriarch on the set. She was very finicky about how she played her part and was given to ordering retakes without consulting the director.

One week the Warrick retakes got out of hand. When it came time to shoot a particularly long scene in which most of us appeared with Ruth, we became so involved in speculating how many takes would be required to satisfy her that we began taking bets on which scene would do the trick. Consequently, when Ruth—obviously not the most secure actress—completed her scene on the first take, she made the mistake of turning to Mia for reassurance. Mia had her money on take three and therefore wrinkled her nose in doubt, suggesting another take. This went on and on until about the fifth take, when the owner of the money on take five—me—cheered Ruth when she was done. Ruth subsequently found out what was going on, exploded, left the set, threatened to call the Screen Actors Guild and report us all, and demanded an apology. She got it. We all felt terrible, not so much because we had bet on her as because we had been found out.

On another occasion there was much preparation for a great love scene I was to play in which I nearly raped poor Rodney Harrington. I grew bored with all the preparation, wandered over to the makeup man, and talked him out of one of the little blood capsules actors put between their teeth and bite into when they're hit to make it appear their mouths are bleeding. I talked him out of two more in the next hour or so and then took up position in front of one of the heavy soundproofed doors which swing inward to allow people to walk onto the soundstage. I had to stand there for several minutes before somebody came through, but when they did I feigned a collision with the door, bit into the capsules, and started screaming. So did several others when they saw the blood flowing from my mouth. I kept up the charade until the studio nurse arrived on the set, and for the next week or so I was the victim of any number of practical jokes. We were jokesters who believed in revenge.

I was also a participant in another scheme which very nearly drove the show's producers and crew crazy. We were spending several days shooting in a courtroom, all of them reaction shots, by which I mean we all sat there pretending to listen, be surprised, stunned, or whatever reaction was called for.

It was slow, boring work and one day when we came back from lunch I noticed that Ryan had combed his hair in a different style. The next morning Mia had changed her hair slightly. This is the sort of thing which drives studio people insane, and Fox—because it had a hit with our show—was trying to make everything letter-perfect. That day after lunch I showed up with my bangs changed. We were all in trouble within two days—the amount of time it takes for the studio to send the film to the lab, view the rushes, plus one day to discover what was wrong. We all caught hell for that one.

During *Peyton Place* Mia had a very public romance with Frank Sinatra, and it wasn't long until it was Mia against the producers, with Mia—not one to be tampered with—the victor. She asked for some time off to be with Frank, was refused, and so she showed up for work the next day with her long blond tresses gone, and a short bob in its place. She absolutely refused to wear a wig. Mia's protest was the talk of the town.

Hair also figured into my affair with Ryan. He was, when he wished to be, an enormously appealing man. Natalie once asked me what kind of lover he was, and I couldn't answer. Even though I had been married twice, I was not experienced enough to know a really good lover when I had one. Ryan, I told her, was like having a glass of champagne without knowing too much about the various brands of champagne. Special, that is, but not a whole lot more. Nor was he wont to keep his complaints to himself.

One morning he rolled over, looked at me, and propped himself up on his elbow. "What do you do to stop that?" he asked, pointing to my hair. It was very long and very curly.

"Stop what?"

"The curling. God, it's awful." Curly hair was not then in fashion, and whatever else he was, Ryan was fashion-conscious. He wasn't one to hesitate when it came to criticizing others, either.

"I straighten it. It takes a while, but it comes out straight."

"Well, you better get up and get going. If you don't straighten it, I'm not taking you to the ballgame with me."

I was hurt and should have followed my instinct to skip the ballgame. I was no great baseball fan, but I had a wish for Ryan to like me, and so I went. We sat with Ryan's chum Lee Majors, who was then single too. When Ryan left his seat to go for a beer and Lee invited me out on a date the next night, I was certain I should have skipped the game. I told Lee I was busy, and told him several more times in the next few weeks before he got the message. At the time he was involved with a super lady named Patty Chandler, and after the two of us became friends I dropped in on her one day. We ate lunch, chatted, and were having a grand time when she looked at her watch, fidgeted, and asked me to leave.

"Lee's coming home and I've got to start dinner. When he's working he doesn't like anybody but me around when he comes home."

That did it for Lee, and Ryan and I didn't last much longer. Natalie, who was aware of our relationship, wondered how it was with Ryan and how, as I recall she put it, he was "fitting into my life."

"Outstanding," I replied.

"Outstanding?"

"Out standing in the hall." Natalie thought that was very funny.

If I have a habit of making the wrong choice of men, I also have a facility for maintaining a friendship after a love affair has ended. Ryan and I continued to be friends until, after I left the series, we went our separate ways. I watched the progress of his affair with Farrah Fawcett, she of the long, lush, curly mane, with interest. I was not at all surprised one day when she appeared, Ryan on her arm, her hair cut short. I should have warned her.

One day I was introduced to Michael Fitzgerald, a writer of some note and a man who had been left money by his Irish family. He was at Fox, working on a couple of TV shows. He was tall, muscular, with sharp features, dark brown hair, and a lovely sense of humor. He was also, like me, forever in a corner somewhere, his nose stuck in a book. He was married, and so we simply became the best of friends, an equation which also, when she wished, included his wife.

In addition to the other things we had in common, we soon discovered we shared a mutual passion: deep-sea fishing. James Brolin and a group of his friends had taken me fishing and I was hooked. I shared my addiction with Natalie, who soon began to be one of a group of people who chartered boats on the weekends and headed out into the Catalina channel.

One night the phone rang and it was Michael. He announced that he and his wife had separated. He wanted to see me. The feeling was mutual. We began a love affair that lasted nearly four years and which even today I look upon as containing some of the happiest moments of my life. He is still married.

20

I stayed with Sandy Webber and *Peyton Place* for two years, until it was finally obvious to us all that Sandy wasn't going anywhere as a character. We experimented with changing her, placing her in somewhat different situations, but Sandy was pretty much played out. Finally it was decided that the character would be written out of the series. I understood and even agreed with the decision, but the idea of leaving the show upset me greatly. It had become an anchor, a place where I knew I had to be every day and where I had a job to do, a job I felt I did very well.

When the last day came, the farewells were tearful and genuine and I went home figuring it was over and glad that at least I had Michael. It was a gradual thing, my falling in love with Michael. There was nothing impetuous about it, nothing particularly adventurous. I was more comfortable with him than with any man I had ever known, particularly so because he was the first to treat me as a smart woman. It was an era of objects, and I had done a good job of turning myself into a desirable one, but with Michael the changes were subtle and, in time, would be permanent.

Once, when he was on a deadline and I was hell-bent for a weekend of fishing, I accepted an invitation to stay with friends at Newport Beach for the weekend. I invited Natalie to go with me. We arrived in Newport late on a Friday night, sneaked in through the back door by prior arrangement, got ready for bed, and discovered we were hungry. We tiptoed into the kitchen, opened the refrigerator, and the only thing we could find to eat was a can of grapefruit sections. We were tired, giddy, and generally not completely sane at the moment, and the sight of grapefruit sections sent us into gales of laughter. We were soon smearing our tears into our mascara, looking like Dracula's daughters, but the laughter would not stop.

We fished the whole weekend, and that next Monday we were both back in town and at work. That afternoon a big pot of freshly planted flowers arrived. They were from Natalie thanking me for the wonderful weekend, and on each flower stem was tied a grapefruit section. It became a joke, a shared secret between us for the rest of her life, a password we used whenever things were wrong and one of us was unhappy, and for a moment it reminded us of a night of untroubled laughter.

A month after I was written out of *Peyton Place*, I got a call inviting me back for a guest shot—one that might develop into a continuing role once again. I was going to be Sandy Webber again, only this time I was returning to town after tramping off to Hollywood. I was to come back wealthy—under mysterious circumstances, of course, the implication being I had grown rich by spending time under any number of powerful men—and swathed in mink. The mink part I liked. I was loyal to the show, too, because it had been very good to me, and so back I went. Sandy took a shot at blackmailing dear, dirty old Mr. Peyton, and that was that. She had nowhere to go but back to Hollywood, and so it was good-bye Sandy forever.

I, meanwhile, had everywhere to go. I had Michael, and he loved to travel. We went to London, to the museums, to auctions at Sotheby's and Christie's, and through endless searches of secondhand bookstores. One, Maxwell Hunley's, was a favorite haunt of his and I was soon one of the regulars too. Michael, who adores first editions, would search the stacks while I would prop myself up in a corner, open a book, and start reading.

Once, when we had argued, I walked into the apartment and found a big bouquet of cut flowers. I am not a fan of cut flowers—they bloom a few days and then they die. He knew this and so I merely glanced at the flowers and wondered if he had forgotten I didn't like them cut. After a while the phone rang. I was Michael.

"Did you get the flowers?"

I issued a perfunctory thank-you.

"Go over to them and look closely." He laughed, and then he hung up.

I looked. Tied on the stem of each flower was a piece of jewelry: little antique bracelets, rings, and pins. Natalie shared my laughter with pieces of grapefruit tied to flowers, Michael shared my love with trinkets. No wonder I loved them both so.

We spent weeks at a time in the south of France, a whole new world to me and one I adored. We stayed in a hotel in St.-Jean-Cap-Ferrat and from there we drove all over the south of France. Michael, who was "officially" separated, introduced me to his many friends, among them David and Hjordis Niven. One night David told a story about a rather grizzled old man he found one day sitting, his easel before him, sketching under a tree on his property. David, who liked privacy and didn't appreciate interruptions of any sort, asked the old man if he'd mind moving on. The man pleaded and cajoled, and David, who had little resistance, agreed to let him paint each morning at the same spot for the next several weeks.

One day, as the agreed-upon time neared an end, there was a knock on the Niven door. It was the old man, come to say thank you. He extended his hand and said, in accented English, how much he'd enjoyed David's pictures. David, every inch the gentleman, claims he shook the man's hand, said thank you, and asked the man's name.

"Marc Chagall," the old man replied. David went about with a red face for a whole day, and then began telling the story on himself. David, as anyone who has read his books knows, is a man who tells a good story.

"I think . . . if I ever left you, and I don't think I could . . . it would only be for someone like David Niven," I said to Michael one night after an uproariously funny evening at the Nivens'.

"Good choice," Michael said. "Good choice."

They were trying times, too. Michael had a young daughter, Tina, whom he adored and often went away to spend time with. Tina lived with her mother, who was present most of the time they were together. His wife, Michael told me, refused his requests for a divorce and from time to time tried to effect a reconciliation. Whenever this happened I'd try to fade into the wallpaper. I was in love, didn't want to be a home-wrecker, and in fact believed Michael when he insisted the end had come long before he'd met me. But it wasn't easy, especially when his sense of family obligation would assert itself.

It asserted itself every family-style holiday, and whenever Christmas rolled around, I'd be an orphan for a couple of weeks, usually through New Year's. There were also summer vacations with his family, weeks when I would feel cut out of his life and unwanted. Michael also had his own puritanical streak to contend with, and one of his hang-ups was that whenever Tina was visiting him in Beverly Hills, I could not be there when breakfast time rolled around. But Michael wanted me there at night, and for many weeks I would set the alarm, get out of bed in the dark, leave by the back door, and be home in my own apartment before Michael and Tina woke up.

It was a concession I was willing to make because I

was in love. The second New Year's Eve we were together—which is to say *not* together, because of the holiday—I went, as usual, to Natalie's black-tie New Year's Eve dinner. Hours before the dinner, she called to inform me that Michael and his wife—who was working on a script she'd got interested in— would be among her guests. I couldn't decide whether to be angry with Michael, who knew I was going to Natalie's, or with Natalie for inviting them in the first place. I was hurt, confused, and lonely, so I dressed myself up and went to Natalie's. I had no- where else to go and Natalie was the person I most wanted to be with, Michael and the Mrs. or not.

It was a complicated time in Natalie's life. Her career was going great guns, her analysis was suc- ceeding, but there wasn't a man in her life, at least not one she could care for as much as I cared for Michael. That, at any rate, is the excuse I fed myself all evening as I watched Natalie watch me be uncom- fortable. She took a sort of perverse pleasure in it, and because she was acting the way she was, I was at home in bed long before midnight, my head buried under the pillow, furious with my own sister. We did not speak for some weeks after that, and when we finally did, the strain took some time to go away. I never asked her why, no doubt out of my lifelong training to avoid troubling Natalie. What I did not understand, and would not understand for some time to come, was that for the first time Natalie was feeling competitive with me. At last I was deeply involved with a decent man who was a success.

Natalie at her best, during the years of her Warner Bros. contract.

Pop took this during a visit to San Francisco. Natalie's pout is out of character—she loved having her picture taken.

My favorite picture of us as children.

Miracle on 34th Street, which has become a classic holiday film. John Payne, Maureen O'Hara, Edmund Gwenn, and the little girl who wouldn't believe in Santa Claus. *(Memory Shop)*

In the early days Mom pulled the strings.

Rehearsing *Rebel Without a Cause*. From the left, Jimmy Dean, Sal Mineo, Corey Allen, and Natalie. Only Corey is still alive.

The "Gigi" look was In.

A publicity shot for *The Searchers*. I played Natalie as a young girl.

With Mom on Van Nuys High School graduation day. She was furious that the studio sent photographers.

Natalie's first wedding to R.J. I wept because I was afraid of losing her.

After the reception Natalie and R.J. proceeded by private train to Florida for the honeymoon.

And then came Warren. By the time *Splendor in the Grass* was released in 1961, they were more than co-stars. *(Wide World Photos)* They looked gorgeous together at the *West Side Story* premiere, but the explosions at home were big ones. *(The Bettmann Archive)*

Natalie was unhappy making *West Side Story*. She couldn't sing, she didn't like her accent, but she thought Richard Beymer was a good sport. *(Memory Shop)*

Mom and Pop at the eighteenth-birthday party Natalie gave for me at the Beverly Hills Hotel. She also gave me a gold satin dress. I felt better than special.

Natalie in one of her striptease costumes for *Gypsy*. Gypsy Rose Lee herself had been her coach. *(The Neal Peters Collection)*

Making *Love with the Proper Stranger* with Steve McQueen. Was it? Natalie wasn't telling. *(The Lester Glassner Collection)*

In *This Property Is Condemned*, a friendship between Robert Redford and Natalie blossomed. *(Memory Shop)*

On the set of *Penelope* she seemed happy for once, but it wasn't so. She attempted suicide shortly after this photo was taken.

Bob & Carol & Ted & Alice. After three years away from acting, Natalie came back with one of the biggest hits of her career. *(The Lester Glassner Collection)*

Richard Gregson and Natalie married in May 1969. Mom announced that it was a bad month for marriages. Mom's on Richard's left; Pop and Norma Crane are beside Natalie.

Natalie with R.J. the second time around. Here she's pregnant with Courtney. The older they got, the better they looked, though Natalie struggled with weight, exercise, pills, drink, and anxiety over not attracting the big film offers.

At Knott's Berry Farm with Kate Wagner, Natasha, and R.J.

On board the *Splendor*, shortly after they bought it. It was on a *Splendor* outing that she died.

With Courtney and Natasha. She was a devoted and loving mother.

At one of Natalie's barbecues. Our reconciliation after a long period of estrangement was complete.

Natalie's Raintree commercial. She had no misgivings about making a commercial. The pay was super and she was only concerned that she look good.

Late that night while I lay in bed crying, the phone rang. It was Michael, apologizing for the whole episode and trying to explain he had come to Natalie's because he wanted to be near me. If that meant bringing her too, so be it. I believed him. I still do.

21

My life with Michael appeared settled and calm compared to Natalie's life. One by one she was dispensing with the people who ran her life, from publicists to accountants. In the mid-1960's she did something that, for Natalie, was simply unprecedented. She got on a plane, all by herself, and flew to New York. She spent several days in a hotel all by herself before coming home.

"I did it! I did it!" she exalted on the phone from New York.

"Terrific," I responded, aware that for Natalie it was something of an accomplishment to go off by herself without one of the coterie that surrounds stars of her stature. "Where all did you go?"

"Bonwit's. Bergdorf's. I bought whatever I wanted, and paid for it with a check. It's really been something."

The notion of Natalie writing a check amused me. Neither of us had the slightest head for numbers, and only Natalie—who had quite a lot of it—had any interest in money. It turned out later that Natalie, who had learned to read the New York Stock Exchange, and had even made a point of visiting her money while she was in New York, did better at watching stocks than she did with her checkbook. Most of the checks she wrote bounced and her business manager had to make good on them. Natalie wasn't one for watching a balance.

Men paraded in and out of her life with a regularity which even she—who was determined to avoid another bad marriage—began to worry about. There had been a South American playboy named Ladislav Blatnik, a big bear of a man whose sources of income —and they must have been considerable, given how he lived—puzzled us all. One night at dinner, Ladislav, in an expansive mood and quite drunk, ate one of Natalie's crystal glasses. We were astonished, and when Ladislav offered to repeat the performance, Natalie, whose crystal was Baccarat, rushed to the kitchen and came back with an ordinary drinking glass. Ladislav, it developed, ate only good crystal.

There was a brief encounter with Tom Courtenay, an actor whose range impressed both of us considerably. He was an easygoing, casual man not at all at home in the world of glamour and stars, and for a while Natalie enjoyed being out of her world too, but before long she was back on the party circuit and Tom was back in England.

Natalie and I developed little rituals in our relationship. We had always enjoyed sitting in front of a mirror and experimenting with makeup, and being grown women with responsibilities of our own did nothing to diminish the pleasure of sitting side by side on Natalie's dressing stool, a sea of tubes and jars open on the table before us. We'd talk as we experimented, never looking directly at one another, but rather talking to each other's reflections. It made candor comfortable, and we could say things we didn't usually attempt face to face.

Jean Leon's La Scala was Natalie's favorite restaurant. It is intimate and elegant, with big red leather booths and counters lined with wine bottles. The food was—and is—excellent, and for many years it was the place to be seen. Natalie had gone there regularly with R.J., and continued to go often throughout the rest of her life. I was frequently with her, especially for one escapade we pulled each winter. It had to be winter because Natalie required a fur coat for this shenanigan and she usually provided me with one too. We'd go to La Scala, eat dinner, have some wine, and shortly before we left, Natalie would reach up behind the booth, grab one of the bottles of expensive wine, and hide it under her arm in her coat sleeve. I'd do the same. We thought it was one of the most adventurous things we did. Natalie, barely hiding her excitement, would sign the bill, and we'd walk—sometimes clanking a bit—out of the restaurant and wait for our car to be brought around.

Natalie occasionally would ask her business manager to send a record of her bills around to the house so that she could take an active part in the financial side of her life and make inquiries of him. She was sitting at home looking over some bills one night and discovered that our dinners at La Scala cost more than her dinners there with other people. Then she made another discovery. We weren't getting away with a thing. Every time we swiped a bottle of wine, it was added to our bill. Jean Leon's sharp waiters had seen it all.

Her life revolved around her career and her analysis, and though she didn't speak often of the analysis, she did make it clear to me how much it meant to her. One night, sitting at her makeup table, I asked how it was going. Natalie, who had been depressed for the previous several weeks, looked up at me and, with tears in her eyes, said: "If it wasn't for the analysis, I'd probably be dead by now. And I've got a long way to go." I pressed her for more, but there was no more to come. Instead, Natalie asked if I'd ever considered getting help. I was already seeing a therapist on a regular basis, so I answered all of her questions and it was clear she was pleased I was seeing someone.

"God knows we need it," she said.

The analysis was so important to her that when Warren literally begged her to take the part opposite him in *Bonnie and Clyde*, she refused. Two months in Texas meant two months of missed sessions. Two months in Texas meant dealing with Warren, too, and Natalie wasn't up to that, either, especially without her psychiatrist. Faye Dunaway, then a virtually unknown actress, got the part. Natalie was not a fan of Faye's, and when a reviewer later referred to Faye as "lantern jaw," Natalie relished the moment.

Warren popped back into her life, but never for

long. What had happened that fateful day several years before was never mentioned, and it was clear when I saw them together that their romance had ended, but that a friendship—"between two survivors" was how Natalie explained it—had emerged. R.J. reappeared too, though in quite a different way. Natalie reacted with carefully controlled dismay when he married Marion Donen, the ex-wife of director Stanley Donen. She wished him well, and meant it, but she also wished him hers once again, if only because Natalie was not one to permit failed relationships, especially a relationship like theirs, whose success—and subsequent failure—was so very public.

Natalie was sitting in her favorite booth in La Scala, having dinner with friends, on the night R.J. and Marion's daughter was born. R.J., the proud father, arrived at the restaurant and began passing out cigars. He passed Natalie's table, looked at her, accepted her congratulations, and then went on. Natalie wanted children, had wanted a child when she was married to R.J., but had accepted his argument that they wait. Now R.J. had a child and she didn't. Natalie, whose composure could be astonishing, proceeded with her dinner, then left and went home alone. It was an unintentionally cruel moment, and it depressed her for weeks afterward.

Her life cheered up considerably when Arthur Loew Jr. appeared on the scene. He was heir to the theater chain and one of those rare, truly funny people. Whenever he was around there was either an interesting conversation or something equally engrossing going on. He was also in love with Natalie, who, in her fashion, loved him back. She was, she said later, not ready to give a whole lot at the time, and she figured her reticence was the cause of their breakup. Still, the times with Arthur were among the best, especially when he was at her side during boring industry functions. He was the perfect date, she said, for the premiere and party of a bad movie, and there are always plenty of those.

One night Natalie gave a party and we were all sitting around talking and drinking, about to launch into what promised to be a long night of playing charades. Natalie's dog wandered into the room, plunked down in the center where all of us could see him, and proceeded to lick his privates. Arthur looked on with detached bemusement.

"If I could do that," he said finally, "I wouldn't have to come to these boring parties." Natalie's shrieks of laughter couldn't be stopped.

Arthur and Natalie got engaged and even lived together for a while, but nothing came of it. He soon went off, married someone else, and moved to Arizona. Natalie talked to him often, and even after she had remarried R.J., went to visit him. It was impossible not to be his friend, even if being his lover had not worked.

David Niven Jr., who has a great deal of his father's easy charm, was on the scene for a while, first with an offer for a picture he wanted to produce and then as Natalie's escort for several months. When Natalie told me it was over, I wasn't at all surprised. I was surprised when he called me a few weeks later and asked me out. As it happened, Michael was off visiting his family, and I accepted David's invitation to dinner. He had in mind a bit more than dinner, but I wasn't interested. I'm glad I wasn't, because Natalie heard we had gone out and was furious with me.

"I thought it was all over between you two," I pleaded with her.

"It is, but that isn't the point."

"What is the point?" I kept asking, but Natalie's point was not made to me. She was angry with me and I honestly began to feel it was all my fault, and so I apologized profusely. She did not telephone, nor did she return my calls for several weeks. When she finally called it was as though nothing had happened.

For some months she dated Richard Johnson, an actor of little note and a socializer of considerable success. Natalie was clearly entranced. Then, along came Richard Gregson.

Richard exuded confidence and worldliness. He was British and had been a successful agent in London before beginning a life of shuttling between England and the United States as a sort of show-business entrepreneur. He produced a few things, put together others, and always had some project going —though just how he did it so well was never clear to any of us, Natalie included. He wasn't nearly as successful as Natalie, at least not by Hollywood standards, but this didn't bother him in the least. The fact that it didn't bother him was a great relief to Natalie. He was a bit older than she, good company, successful, and he quickly fell in love with her. She resisted briefly, but his timing was right, and before long, Natalie and Richard were engaged.

We were having a congratulatory drink, just the two of us, and I made some joke about Natalie assigning her leftover men to me. She laughed and said there really weren't any, that her choice had really been between Richard Johnson and Richard Gregson.

"How did you decide?"

"I've already slept with Richard Gregson," she said, fingering her engagement ring. Richard Gregson was it.

"There's got to be more to it than that." I tried not to sound too surprised.

"Oh, there's more besides that. He isn't intimidated by who I am."

He certainly wasn't, and though the fact that Natalie had already become his lover—a consideration for marriage among her contemporaries, and particularly so in our family—was certainly important to her, it was just one of several factors. Natalie had been engaged several times before, but we all knew this one was going on to what Natalie jokingly called "phase two." When she was with Richard, Natalie was settled, calm, and happy.

Their marriage in 1969 was one of the happiest in all our lives. They had a big Russian Orthodox wedding and the only one who was concerned was Mom. May is a bad month for marriages, she told everyone —including Natalie. May brides cry a great deal, she said, but Natalie had long ago learned to ignore Mom's superstitions.

They moved into a big house in Bel Air and quickly settled into life as one of the most popular couples in the business. His business and her career occasionally necessitated long separations, but they seemed not at all bothered by them. Not being bothered, at least on Natalie's part, was a pretense. We were sitting on the floor of her living room one day when Richard was in London on a long trip. Richard called and Natalie and he spoke for several minutes, chatting about business and household matters, and Natalie kept saying she missed him. She was suddenly vulnerable and lonely, and I could see the tears in her eyes. When she hung up, she gave her head a shake, took a deep breath, and went on with our conversation as though nothing had happened. I sat there astonished once again at her remarkable control.

It is an irony in both our lives that we were raised to be beautiful, glamorous women—Mom's term, not mine—and we both turned out to be our happiest in conventional marriages with kids and all the other clichés people like us are supposed to avoid. Natalie loved the institution of marriage, and so do I, even after all my lack of success with it.

While Natalie was taking marriage seriously, she was also spoofing it in *Bob & Carol & Ted & Alice*, a movie which genially savaged the institution of marriage.

Natalie was on home territory, and her only worry was doing comedy. She was uncomfortable with comedy and felt no instinct for it. But she did trust her director, and Paul Mazursky provided Natalie—and Elliott Gould, Dyan Cannon, and Robert Culp—with a nearly perfect movie. Natalie's other concern besides doing comedy was Dyan Cannon. Dyan was then and is now a strong, uninhibited lady with a great sense of herself and her talent. Natalie, who was a contemporary but was really from a different era, was envious of her and worried Dyan would come off better in the movie than she.

Natalie need not have worried. *Bob & Carol & Ted & Alice* was a big hit, and it put Natalie back on top after an absence from the screen of nearly three years. Unlike so many other times in her life when she was unable to truly enjoy her success, this time Natalie relished every minute of it.

She now had everything she had wanted, except for one thing, and she was going to get that, too.

She was just over three months pregnant when she called me and asked me to bring my friend Judy Weiss over to talk with her about raising children. Natalie and I both admired Judy. She had married young, had three children, worked to put her husband through medical school, and had finally settled into life as a doctor's wife. That, of course, is when he asked for a divorce. Judy not only raised three remarkable children, she also started several successful businesses. That she had managed both motherhood and a career appealed mightily to Natalie.

"I want to ask her a lot of questions," Natalie said.

"First about babies, then how to deal with the working-mother thing. I want to know all about that."

"You chose the right lady," I said. Two days later Judy and I arrived at Natalie's house. I knew the moment we arrived that something was wrong. Natalie, whose enthusiasm at the time knew no bounds, was formal and stiff when she greeted Judy. To make things more informal, I suggested we all sit down on the floor.

Natalie chatted briefly with me, but she pointedly ignored Judy. Judy, who knew only the friendly, open Natalie, looked at me, obviously puzzled. I shrugged and plowed on:

"Now, about your questions, Natalie . . ."

"What questions, Lana?"

We sat in awkward silence for a few moments until Judy plunged into a dissertation on pregnancy, beginning with how good Natalie looked. Natalie gazed at the ceiling with the look of tried patience one has when suffering a great bore. Then she got up and excused herself.

"I've got to make a phone call. Make yourselves comfortable, I may be a while," she said as she walked out of the room.

"I don't know, Judy. I really don't know. Honest, she did call and ask to have you come over."

"Well, she won't have to ask me to leave," Judy said, gathering her things. I left with her.

I have no idea what happened, no idea what preceded the meeting, or what was on Natalie's mind while it was going on. True to my conditioning as a star's sister, I never asked Natalie for an explanation and Natalie never volunteered anything that might clear up her unusual behavior. Natalie called me less than a week later and chatted on as though the incident had never occurred.

Natasha Gregson was born on September 29, 1970. With Natasha, Natalie discovered something else she was very good at. She adored being a mother, became an energetic supporter of the La Leche League, and for the next three years life in the Gregson household revolved around Natasha.

22

While Natalie settled into marriage and motherhood, I led a very different sort of life. I was forever going hither and yon with Michael, or in pursuit of him. We alternated between Los Angeles, London, the south of France, and sometimes Paris.

It was a tumultuous time because it seemed that whenever Michael and I had everything running smoothly, something would cause a major disruption. That something more often than not was his wife. She still withheld the divorce, still demanded his attention.

Michael was in the midst of a tug of war with his conflicting loyalties and had nearly postponed my trip the day after I was to fly to Paris, change planes, and go on to the south of France to meet him. The trip was on, then off, then on. I refused a picture to be with him, and with each postponement my anger increased. Finally, in the course of a telephone conversation during which he changed his mind twice, the date was set. With Mom and Pop in tow to see me off, I arrived at the airport and was shown to the Pan

Am lounge. Robert Evans and Ali MacGraw were also there. I had dated Bob years before, and we ran into one another from time to time, so as I entered, he waved at me. Ali, whom I had never met, looked up suspiciously, then calmly set fire to the newspaper Bob was reading. He looked absolutely astonished and we all started laughing. They were newly married and Ali, it appeared, was given to small fits of jealously and humor. The next person who came into the lounge was Alain Delon. He was, as any number of women have said before and since, quite simply the most beautiful man I had ever seen.

The four of us arranged to sit together on the plane, and we had a grand time getting to Paris. I had the best time of all. I was engaged in a flirtation which I truly enjoyed, and which Alain responded to immediately. When we were about two hours from Paris he leaned over and whispered an invitation into my ear, an invitation to join him in his bedroom in Paris immediately after the plane landed. I equivocated—not much, but enough to see how determined he was—before saying yes.

I had no sooner agreed than I began to feel guilty. Here I was, flying off to meet the man I loved. I was angry with him, jealous of his attention to his wife, furious over her demands. I was also being tempted by a man widely known for his abilities as a lover. It was a mixture of revenge and lust on my part, and I understood it rationally if not emotionally, and I succumbed.

For two days Alain and I were alone in Paris, making love, walking from café to café, shop to shop. It was, finally, all too much for me and so I left and went to Voile d'Or in Cap-Ferrat, where Michael was waiting. I explained I had been in Paris "with friends" for two days, trying to decide what to do about the two of us. He did not believe me, though he pretended he did. He pretended for less than a day. That's when Alain telephoned and had me paged. Alain wanted to say thank you and to say he wanted to continue the relationship. Michael was sullen and jealous, and I felt a terrible guilt. A guilt made worse by the fact that I wanted to be with Alain as much as I wanted to be with Michael.

We parted. I stayed behind and Michael went home to New York. I told him it was time he made a decision. I wanted to marry him and spend the rest of my life as Mrs. Michael Fitzgerald, and though I had made this perfectly clear over the previous years, I said it once again—carefully, because I didn't want to win him by pressure or threats. He'd had enough of that already.

I went to Rome and spent a couple of days with Bob and Ali, and in the course of tramping from ruin to museum with the indefatigable Ali, we struck up a friendship. She was bright, funny, a talented artist, outspoken, and not at all sure about her acting career. She wanted the fame and the attention, but she wasn't sure of her abilities as an actress. We talked a great deal those several days and when I came back to Los Angeles it was with a renewed sense of purpose and independence. I didn't even go back to

Paris and Alain, though he asked me twice. I came home instead.

It was late summer, and I spent a couple of days at the beach with Natalie, Natasha, and Richard; then I went back to the apartment I seemed always to be leaving, and began to put my life in order. I called my agent and announced I wanted to go back to work. Once again I was ready to resume a career I had never wanted, then wanted, then abandoned after the success of *Peyton Place*, turning my back on a pile of scripts and job offers. Michael had paid for all my traveling, and so there was still a good supply of *Peyton Place* money left. I had time, for once, to sit down and think about the future. Michael came, Michael went, and we lived with his dilemma.

One day, before Michael left for New York and his family, I told him it was either his wife or me, that I'd be waiting no more. He was stunned by the simple directness of my statement and he knew I meant it. I think he believed I meant it more than I did. I was certain I'd give in again if he came back to me. He left without making up his mind.

I got even, not out of spite but out of a deep desire to make Michael so jealous he'd come rushing back to me. He was no sooner gone than Alain telephoned from New York, inviting me to come to visit him for several days. I thought a few days on the town with Alain the perfect antidote to cheer me up and to drive Michael insane with jealousy.

Unlike Michael's invitations, Alain's did not include a plane ticket. I bought myself a tourist ticket

and Mom and Pop came along to see me off. Mom
always accompanied Natalie and me to the airport; it
was something she seemed somehow to need and so
we both routinely marched her into the airport with
us. On the plane, I sat down, fastened my seat belt,
and found myself sitting next to a hippie. I had never
seen a hippie up close and I was fascinated and
frightened. For someone who had done a lot and
been many places, I had still led a fairly sheltered life,
certainly a life where hippies were looked upon with
extreme disapproval. Then, something snapped.

Without knowing why or even understanding any
of what was happening, I got up and walked off the
plane. I got off and on, then off again. I was in a state
of incomprehensible panic. To add to my extreme
indecision, there was a mechanical problem with the
plane itself and so I sat in the airport trying to decide
what to do, and while I tried to get control of myself,
the plane waited. Mom and Pop had left as soon as
they saw me get on board, so I had no one to turn to
in my quandary.

How much did I want Michael? A lot. More than
anything. What could I do to get him? Nothing. I
knew he'd hear Alain and I were in New York almost
as soon as we turned up together, but I didn't want to
hurt him. I did want to make him jealous. I sat there
staring at the plane, trying to make up my mind
whether or not to go. Finally the prospect of the start
of the holidays alone once again was too much. I got
on the plane and went to New York.

I was back home a week later. The time in New

York with Alain had been romantic and, in its way, exciting, but it was not for me. Michael telephoned after the holidays and we arranged to meet. To his credit he had made a decision and wanted to explain it in person. He was staying with his marriage. He loved me and would always love me, he said, but his commitment to his wife and his daughter was something he felt he had to honor. I listened and finally told him that it was his sense of commitment and honor I admired most about him, and that it was ironic that those two qualities would be what took him away from me.

Natalie, of course, followed the whole Michael experience with great interest, and even went so far as to help me scheme to get him to marry me. She shared my frustration, but was—finally—impatient for it all to end. She, more than I, realized it could not be resolved the way I wanted.

"He won't do it," she insisted on one of the occasions Michael left his wife. "He won't stay away."

"Maybe this time," I said, hoping against hope.

"It's a bet I'd be happy to make, but only if I lose," she said.

From the snug comfort of her marriage, Natalie watched as I floundered, and when I needed moral support, she was there. She could hardly suppress her curiosity after I told her about Alain.

"God, I wish we were twins," she said.

"Why?"

"So I could take your place for just one night."

When I finally made the break from Michael, Natalie telephoned daily for the first few weeks, determined that my resolve remain strong. Michael said at that time that we would always be a part of one another's lives and that we'd always talk to one another, but I didn't really believe him. And for a while I was right. Then one day, many months later, the phone rang and it was him. We made a date for lunch and had a wonderful time together. He has been a part of my life and we have been friends ever since.

23

Our lives formed a sharp contrast during these years: Natalie, married and a mother; me, wishing for both while at the same time trying to have a good time, too. Sometimes the settled nature of her life upset her, and when it did I tried to sense her unrest and not to say too much about my own life. I could not conceive of Natalie being jealous of me, but there was an occasional edge to her which made me uncomfortable.

She and Richard had a house at Lake Tahoe, and they invited me and the young agent I was dating to come up for a week. Actually, the invitation came to me, and he was included as an afterthought—and I should have taken the hint right there. He and I moved into the guest room, and we were careful not to disturb the status quo. I had been there less than a day when I sensed Natalie was bored and a bit irritable, but when I asked her what was wrong she shrugged off my question and said I was imagining things. The next day she brought Natasha into the guest bathroom to give her a bath in the sink, which,

Natalie said, was bigger than the sink in her bedroom. I rushed in to watch the happy ritual just as Natalie, biting her lip in grim concentration, sent a load of bathwater sloshing over my makeup and my birth-control pills.

"Oh my God, my birth-control pills," I said, and reached to try to save them.

"You shouldn't leave things like that lying around," Natalie snapped, sending more water flying. And she said no more. My friend and I left a day later—he pretended to have been called back to town for business—and Natalie waved us away as if nothing had happened.

"I don't understand why she did that," he said on the trip home.

"I'm sure it was an accident," I apologized. In my mind I could hear Mom, her voice superimposed over my own: "Don't upset Natalie. Whatever you do, don't upset Natalie."

While Natalie gave her all to mothering, I was beginning to write verse. It began as a form of therapy, suggested by the therapist I was seeing at the time. Then it evolved into a terrific way of passing time on airplanes. It was also, and this is what appealed to me most, a means of putting a sharp focus on a sprawling and confused life—mine. The verses were my attempt to find my niche in life, written with no thought of publication, but rather as an attempt to clarify my feelings. I kept my notebook with me at all times. The poems tended to be much like their author—searching and, sometimes, cynical:

The white unfinished
wall that stands
marked only with
patches
of time
cobwebs
of short experiences
of life
fingerprints
of a few
who have tried to
touch
But still empty
and waiting
waiting
for the man
with a full mind
of pictures
who will bring
with him
his colored ideas
and slowly
with soft hands
and deliberate strokes
will draw the warmth
of freedom
and love
upon my mind.

That was the romantic side of me. There was another one, too:

I would have turned down my
bed, but I didn't get any
better offers.

Finally, I had a book of them and I used the verse above as my title. That book done, I started work on another, work that was interrupted by a catastrophic event in Natalie's life.

Word had reached me that there was trouble in Natalie and Richard's paradise, but I just chalked it up to the usual show-business gossip and to envy over Natalie's obviously happy and successful marriage. I know I was envious, so I assumed everyone else was too. Natasha was a year old, an apple-cheeked darling trying to walk and already talking a bit. She was the center of Natalie's life.

Natalie came home from lunch one day and accused Richard of infidelity. What transpired in those first few hours after her accusation is now known only to Richard, Natalie's analyst, and possibly R.J. I would imagine Natalie was nearly hysterical with rage, for she was not one to be scorned in any matter without reacting forcefully. She was also, and of this I'm certain, deeply and seriously unhappy, her safe, secure world destroyed. Some women, after an initial anger, accommodate themselves to husbands like Richard. I think, given my own experience and the experience of friends, most forgive. Not Natalie.

She told Richard to leave, and he did. Natalie was not much over five feet tall but she had a strength—physical and moral—which was formidable when aroused.

For the first few days Natalie refused to see anybody. She had to be tranquilized, she needed pills to sleep, and she roused herself only for Natasha. Finally she saw her lawyers. Then she saw me.

I drove up to the house and went upstairs to Natalie's beautiful bedroom, with its flowered wallpaper, huge bed and chaise lounges, and the dressing table and mirrors where we had spent so much time. I had come on a mission of sorts, one that Mom and I had planned. I was, as usual, the devil's advocate.

I hugged her and told her how sorry I was, and she began crying. We sat on the edge of her bed while I handed her Kleenex. She told me what had happened, though by now I had heard it all, and so had just about everybody else in Hollywood. It was one thing—and not at all unusual at that—to accuse your husband of infidelity. It was quite another to order him out of the house and end a marriage everybody looked to as an example.

I had come to give comfort and also to suggest— very carefully—that Natalie reconsider, that she look upon this incident as a reaction to a stressful time in their marriage. After all, Natalie's life had been given almost exclusively to her baby, and a bit of the glamorous edge of being married to a movie star had worn off for Richard. He was a man who liked excitement, and Natalie was no different, really—it was just that she had taken time out for something else. Mom and I had talked it over carefully, and we wanted to plant the notion of reconciliation and let it take its course. I explained all this to Natalie, being careful not to tell her that Mom and I had talked it over. I omitted Mom because if Natalie was going to fly into a fury, I didn't want her being angry at her own mother at a time she might be needing her.

Fury is what Natalie felt.

"You don't understand, do you," she said, and her look could have killed. "You don't really understand who I am, do you." It wasn't a question, it was a statement.

"Of course I do. I only meant to suggest there might be another side to all of this. Maybe he needed more attention from you."

"What the hell does that mean?"

"Natalie. I'm on your side. All the way. I just hate to see you getting a divorce. That's probably the one thing I know better than you now. I'm merely suggesting you consider a reconciliation along with all the other possibilities you're considering."

"There is only one possibility. One."

Then her fury turned to rage.

"Did Richard send you? Did that son-of-a-bitch talk you into coming here and saying this?"

"Absolutely not." It took a few minutes, but I think she finally believed me. I had made a big tactical blunder, and so I decided to throw my tank into reverse and back out of the situation before I did any more damage.

Natalie's wound, and her desire for revenge, was such that she made it clear to anyone and everyone that Richard had betrayed one of the finest, most loved people in the business. True enough. She stopped short of putting up roadblocks around all of Beverly Hills, but friends of Natalie's dealt with Richard at their own peril. Richard moved back to London.

I came back later that same day with Mom—that was when Mom made her lunge for Natalie's wedding ring—hoping Mom could reason with her a bit. Mom agreed with everything Natalie said, and I stood by and said nothing, but it was clear by now I'd caused my sister to get angry with me by attempting to reason with her. I stayed nearby, but for some time to come I was persona non grata at Natalie's house. I waited several months and nothing happened. Natalie did not call; Mom carefully omitted any references to her when she called. Mom was now afraid to bring up the subject and desperately worried I'd tell Natalie what I'd done wasn't my idea only. Finally I asked Mom to arrange a reconciliation and she suggested we wait awhile.

Instead, I wrote Natalie a note and sent it with a bunch of flowers. It was an apology for something I told her I'd done with the best of intentions. I got a thank-you note back, not a particularly warm one. Natalie understood, she said, but there was no hint of forgiveness in the note.

I waited a couple more months and asked Mom to intercede. This time she agreed, and one day the telephone rang and it was Natalie. She was having a small dinner party and would I come?

"Would I?"

Natalie was beginning to emerge once again. She went out occasionally for lunch, and to infrequent dinner parties at night. She did not date for many months, and then she took care that it wasn't public. Mart Crowley, who had stood by her through so much, was once again on hand, his wit—which can be delightfully wicked—keeping things lively. Mart and Tommy Thompson remained two of her closest friends. Tommy, after writing a string of best-sellers, died—young and tragically—of cancer within a year after Natalie died. Mart is now the producer on *Hart to Hart*, a position both he and I sought, and for which Natalie and R.J. arranged for him to be chosen. It caused some awkward moments between us, but our friendship survived. The day Mart was made producer of *Hart to Hart*, Natalie looked up and smiled her best innocent smile. Mart is a man who thinks nothing of spending a small fortune on his clothes, and this was not lost on Natalie. "Now Mart can afford to dress the way he's dressed all of his life," she quipped.

At the time of Natalie's divorce from Richard, Mart was a successful playwright having a terrible time getting another play written. He was present at one of Natalie's dinners, and among the other guests— probably ten in all—was Jerry Brown, California's young bachelor governor. Mart immediately whispered the news: Natalie and Jerry were dating but keeping it a secret. I waited until Natalie headed for the bathroom and followed her. I was delighted she was dating someone and told her so.

Natalie just giggled, and so I pressed her. "He's nice," she said, "but he's boring. For a while I thought it was me, but it's not."

"Well, listen, enjoy it while it lasts. And do me a favor?"

"What?"

"Don't sit me next to him at dinner."

Natalie wasn't much for jokes—she couldn't tell them well and didn't have that sort of sense of humor. She did, however, love mischief and was not above the occasional practical joke.

I sat next to Jerry Brown at two dinner parties in a row, with Natalie looking up and smiling innocently whenever I shot her a dirty look. Mart, who knew what was going on, didn't help. He was on my other side at one dinner and made sure I had plenty of time to talk to the governor without Mart interrupting. He would let me know he was there by jabbing me occasionally with his elbow. I came to know Jerry Brown as serious and dedicated and, yes, a bit boring.

The rift over my suggestion that a reconciliation with Richard at least be considered finally ended after several months. Mom called one day to say Natalie wanted me to drop by and say hello. As usual, the invitation to reappear did not come from Natalie herself and, as usual, I complied. I brought up the subject of her anger, intending to apologize, as Natalie and I tried to fill ourselves up on a tiny clump of cottage cheese and an even tinier one of tuna fish. We were both dieting, Natalie with her usual determination, me with my usual small appetite. She waved away my apology, obviously not wanting to discuss the subject.

One day the two of us went shopping at Bullock's

Wilshire. Natalie, although she adored clothing, was not much of a shopper. Clothes were usually brought to the house and she'd make her choices and then send the rest back. This time, though, she decided a morning of shopping followed by lunch might be fun, and invited me along. Her mission, it turned out, was to find pillows for the two sofas in her living room.

We hit a couple of the expensive boutiques in Beverly Hills and found nothing, so off we went to Bullock's, a department store where movie stars are seldom seen. Natalie and I were wearing large dark glasses, *de rigueur* in the California sunshine. We made our way through the dress department and the cosmetics department, where as usual we both bought more than we needed. Then Natalie came upon a display in the clothing section where a mannequin was seated on a chair. Behind the chair were two pillows made of precisely the color and fabric Natalie was searching for. She approached one saleslady and was dismissed, went after another who picked up a telephone and ignored her. Natalie, who was accustomed to attention, was irked—not a petulant, nasty anger, but a sort of bemused irritation about what to do next.

"They don't recognize you," I whispered as Natalie picked up another pillow and examined it. Finally we were told to go to another department to pay for them. This we did, only to be told that since the pillows had been removed from a display, the saleslady needed the approval of her manager, who, of course, had left for the day. Natalie suddenly got a wicked gleam in her eye.

"C'mon. Follow me," she said. With that she handed me her two bags of cosmetics, clutched two pillows to her chest, looked at the selection and grabbed a third, then turned and started out of the store.

"Natalie," I whispered, trotting to keep up. "What'll you do if they stop you at the door?"

"I'll tell them that if they expect me to pay for these pillows they ought to have a saleslady around."

Natalie made it out the door and onto the street before breaking into a run. I was right behind her. We abandoned our diets for lunch and had wine to celebrate our great adventure.

24

In 1970, I did it. I'd been asked before and had always resisted, but this time when Hugh Hefner and his people approached me to pose for *Playboy*, I was willing to consider the possibility. My change of heart came one day as I was having a friendly, casual lunch with Michael. He thought the idea absolutely super and insisted it'd be a great boost in a career which had been slow to inactive due to my own inertia. It was time to get it all going again, he insisted, and more than that, time to make some money. That last part was becoming painfully clear.

My tentative yes produced the photographer Mario Casselli, sent to do the final persuading and to put me at my ease. He did just that. He was warm and amiable and absolutely insisted that taking my clothes off for him and his camera would not embarrass me in the least. And so it was agreed, and Michael provided his house. It was a place, he said with a smile, where I had taken off my clothes before and so I didn't have that to worry about.

I decided to consult Natalie, then changed my

mind. It seemed at first unfair to ask her to help me make a decision like this, and I was concerned too that she might disapprove or maybe even feel threatened by a form of competition in which she—for her own reasons—would never become involved. Natalie was uncomfortable with nudity, an attitude that had more to do with the mores of her particular generation than it had to do personally with her. She had stood up in a bathtub in *Splendor in the Grass* but had not really been nude; still it had made her so self-conscious that she had refused a retake and had never done anything like it again. I wasn't as self-conscious as Natalie and I had a somewhat different attitude toward appearing nude. I was only slightly less conservative than Natalie on the subject, but I was also approaching the problem from a very different perspective. I talked all of this over with Michael, and he agreed. Natalie would be told after the fact.

Mario, and I suppose the other *Playboy* photographers too, had learned that the business of posing nude should be made as easy and as pleasurable— even sensual—as possible. Everything was ready when I arrived, and instead of merely accepting the fact that I had taken off my clothes, Mario regarded me admiringly. He made me, and what I was doing, an occasion. Given the fact that for most of the pictures I was wearing nothing more than a shawl, this was a relief. I posed in any number of near-costumes, and to this day I think the most provocative picture in the bunch is one in which I'm completely covered by a fitted lace dress which even covers my arms down

to my wrists. It was the dress Natalie had chosen for
me and her other bridesmaids to wear for her marriage to Richard. In my other favorite I'm wearing
Michael's cat, a friendly animal who had always preferred my lap to his master's.

The session took most of the day, and it was actually a pleasurable experience. I've talked to others
who've posed for *Playboy* and my impression of their
experience is that they found it a very narcissistic and
sensual experience. I found it sensual, but not at all
narcissistic. On the contrary, I felt I was posing to
give pleasure to Mario. That, perhaps, accounts for
the fact that I was so at ease during the whole session.
It must be so, for it was something I'd never done
before and have never done since, except for appearing seminude in a couple of films, and by this time
nudity of every sort was commonplace in films.

I had no misgivings at all until I saw the pictures.
Then I panicked. I telephoned Natalie to tell her
what I'd done, and her first response was dead silence and her second was, "I see."

"I think the pictures are very tasteful, but I just
don't know if it's a good idea. When I did it I was
convinced it was a good idea. Michael thinks it's a
terrific idea."

"Michael would."

"They're in good taste. I made sure of that."

"I'm sure they're absolutely yummy."

I gave up on that conversation fast. Then I telephoned Mom, and she thought it was a good idea
because it would show me at my best, or some words

to that effect. When I asked her if Natalie would do anything like that, she said, "Absolutely not! She doesn't have to."

Natalie's response angered me, and Mom's infuriated me. I called up Hugh Hefner and begged him not to run the pictures. I told him the truth: that I dreaded offending my sister, and for that reason alone I had changed my mind. At that point Michael intervened, and as usual he had a splendid idea for working it all out. He suggested I submit my book of poetry to Hefner and say that, if the magazine was willing to publish my poetry, it could publish the nude pictures too. I felt it was worth a try, and packed the poetry off to Chicago and the *Playboy* headquarters.

Natalie continued to register her disapproval by silence. I am not sure what it is that causes years of acquiescence to turn to defiance. I know only that the longer Natalie's silence went on, the more upset I got. When Hefner called and said he would print a number of my poems with the pictures, I gave my consent. Defiantly.

The pictures appeared in the issue of April 1971. I feel that the poetry surrounding them bares more of me than the pictures do. By *Playboy*'s standards today, they are very chaste pictures—only my breasts are bared, though I am nude in several of the pictures and artfully covered in most places. They caused a small sensation in Hollywood, for it was still not the time when actresses were baring all for *Playboy*.

Natalie made her disapproval known to everybody, but not to me. I heard from any number of mutual friends that she thought it had been a bad idea from the start. The subject came up at any number of Natalie's dinner parties, where her displeasure was immediately made known and, within hours, relayed to me by one or another of her guests. There is a postscript to Natalie's reaction, one that does not really surprise me much and one that certainly explains the clever workings of the *Playboy* empire. Natalie's disapproval eventually came to Hefner's attention, and he responded by launching a campaign. A campaign that nearly worked. He decided Natalie should pose for *Playboy* too. Hefner and his persuaders went to work. Natalie, a mother and once again a single woman, was tempted, if only to prove she was still in good shape. There was a big *if* to Natalie's agreement. Edith Head must provide all of the clothing, custom-made for Natalie. *Playboy* quickly contacted Miss Head, and then went reeling off in shock when they heard her price. There were some subsequent negotiations, but between Miss Head's price and Natalie's demand that she be given the cover— unprecedented at the time, a precedent broken some years later by Barbra Streisand—it all proved too much for Hefner and his people. The subject was dropped. All of this was told to me by Mario, who had no reason to tell anything but the truth. It was a subject never mentioned by Natalie, and even if she had brought it up, I wouldn't have known what to say.

The pictures also did what Michael promised: they gave me a better than good career boost. Cubby Broccoli, who was about to begin shooting what was being touted as Sean Connery's final James Bond film, *Diamonds Are Forever,* telephoned and asked me to play Bond's girlfriend, Plenty O'Toole. Me, who had spent so many of my high-school years with my nose buried in Ian Fleming's Bond adventures. Not only that, but the pay was terrific. Within weeks I was packed and ready to leave.

The film was shot mostly in Las Vegas, and I decided to bring along my pet cat for company at night. I was not the nightclub sort any longer and I have never had any interest in gambling. Besides, on films you're up early and the days are long. So, along she came. I got off the plane, counted my luggage, found the driver who'd been sent to meet me, and off we went to the hotel. How I did it I'll never know, but as I got out of the limousine to walk into the hotel, I reached in through the wire netting to stroke my cat, whose complaining was now getting quite loud and insistent. My finger got stuck; looking as though I was wrapped around the cat carrier, I made my entrance.

I was sure that once I could sit down and open the cage, I would work my finger out of it. I also had a pair of cuticle cutters in my baggage which could be used to snip a piece of the wire. All I needed was to get to my suite—a suite was what had been offered and so it was what I expected—and I'd get everything taken care of. The room clerk, with great embarrassment, explained that my room would not be ready for two more hours, but that I was to use Mr. Connery's suite, which was on the same floor, until mine was ready.

"Where is Mr. Connery?" I asked.

"Not in just now," the clerk said. The shooting had not yet started and I figured Sean must be off doing something or other and that it'd be okay to wait in his suite. I was handed a key and off I went, assured my luggage would be placed in my suite.

It didn't occur to me to knock or to otherwise announce myself. I simply unlocked the door and walked right in.

"Well, hello there!" Sean Connery boomed at me. He was stark naked and sitting on the toilet. I let out a shriek. He stood up, smiled, and said, "Don't be frightened. I'll be right out. Put your animal carrier down anywhere you'd like."

"I can't."

"What do you mean, you can't?" He was still standing there facing me, and I quickly turned away.

"My finger's stuck in the damn thing."

He laughed, closed the door, and finished his business. When he came out a few minutes later he was wearing a bathrobe and a conspiratorial grin. I couldn't help laughing. It was a memorable meeting. Sean eventually got my finger extracted from the cage and provided a bandage to wrap around the cut I got forcing it out. He invited me out to dinner that evening and I went. He invited me back to his room to read over our lines and I declined.

Sean is the most masculine of men, extremely confident, and when he wants, very charming and attentive. For the next several days I got the best of Sean Connery—something I hadn't expected because I'd been warned that he was weary of James Bond and tended to be difficult and demanding on the pictures. We joked on the set, worked well together, and at night we went out to dinner together, always trying to find a place where we wouldn't be seen.

It was just a matter of time, and I figured "Why not?" I had no reason to decline and every reason to say yes. He was an assured lover, given to bursts of spontaneity. Once, returning from a hard day on the set, he came rushing at me as soon as we got to his hotel room. He had his clothes off and was helping me out of mine when I hugged him and got a whiff of Sean after a day of physical exertion. He smelled like the bottom of a lion's cage and did not appreciate my insistence he take a shower first.

Our relationship was less a romance than it was an interlude. The rigors of making the picture—the Bond films are as hard on the actors as they appear to be on screen—coupled with Sean's by now tumultuous relationship with the director and producers, took its toll. It seems to me as I remember it that Sean had made some exorbitant demand for another Bond film after *Diamonds* and had been flatly turned down by Cubby Broccoli, an expansive man whose family name had been assigned when his father immigrated to the United States and informed the authorities he was a broccoli farmer. Cubby could be tough, and so could Sean. The encounter was being given much publicity, and it was not long before a very public search was under way for the "new" James Bond. Sean and Cubby eventually parted, not friends, and it would be more than a decade before Sean would play Bond again—and even then it wouldn't be for Cubby. Roger Moore already had the big salary.

I wore spit curls in part of the picture because I was playing with my cat one night and she scratched my cheek, a scratch bad enough so that it was impossible to cover with makeup. I also had one particular scene I dreaded, and Sean knew it—I'd told him so repeatedly. He said he'd be there when I did it, and that did much to alleviate my fear.

The scene was this: clad only in a pair of skimpy bikini underpants, my character was to be thrown through the window of a hotel room a number of stories off the ground and plummet into the swimming pool. To give the illusion of falling, it would be impossible to dive. So a tall platform was built beside the pool and Dick Butler took over. He is a wonderful man who was stunt coordinator on the picture and one of those professionals who won't take a chance unless he knows exactly what is involved. He also knows when his performers are frightened, and I was flat out terrified.

Terrified for two reasons. One, the fall itself. Two, the fact that I'd be nearly nude and hundreds of people would be standing around watching—not just the crew but anybody staying at the hotel who hap-

pened to wander by would see what was going on. I
waited for Sean to show up, and when he didn't, I got
so nervous the wardrobe girl took pity on me and
went out and bought a bottle of blackberry brandy,
which we proceeded to sip throughout the evening.
To reassure me about the crowds, I was told there
would be few people other than crew watching because the shot was being made in the small hours of
the morning.

I was wearing a terry-cloth robe when I climbed
the platform. Dick was up there waiting. My first
great shock was that the place was full of people. I
had been told there wouldn't be many so that I'd
calm down. This was Las Vegas, and the small hours
of the morning are the busiest part of the day. I was
on display. I turned my back to the crowd, took off
my robe, and looked down and saw Sean standing on
the edge of the crowd. I shot him a pleading look and
he smiled back at me. Dick, as we'd planned it,
helped me up on his shoulders and I stayed there
until I had my cue to fall. Dick talked steadily, reassuring me it'd all go well, telling me how to fall
straight, then roll slightly as I hit the water so that I'd
not belly-flop and hurt myself. When the order came,
Dick sent me flying.

The wardrobe people were there with a robe when
I climbed out of the pool, and there was much applause. I was elated that it was over, and my elation
lasted about a minute, because it was decided a retake would be necessary. It took some time to get
ready, because my hair had to be dried, my makeup

reapplied, and, needless to say, more blackberry brandy consumed. Sean stopped by to say it looked spectacular and I peevishly reminded him he'd promised to come and be with me before the jump. He offered no apology and soon wandered off.

The second fall was even more successful than the first, and as soon as it was done, I headed back to my suite, had a bowl of soup, and fell into an exhausted sleep. I was no sooner asleep than there was a knock at my door. It was Sean. He wanted to come in. As politely as I could, and trying to hide my unhappiness that he hadn't been there as he'd said, I refused. I was simply too tired for company just as the sun was coming up.

The next morning, Sean ignored me when I'd speak to him on the set. It was especially humiliating because I assumed by now everybody in the company knew we were having an affair. I had one week left to work on the picture and during that time the only exchanges between Sean and me occurred on camera. He did not speak to me again. We did not see one another for several more years, and when next we met, the circumstances—and the results—would be very different.

25

I tended to bounce from one film to another, to move without hesitation between film and television. Acting was my work, no more, no less. Natalie, however, was a star. She could not bounce, she had to make the right decisions.

She had become a star and had been one for a number of years before she even knew what it meant. She once said she didn't really become aware of what a star was until she'd made *Miracle On Thirty-fourth Street*. She was eight when it was made. Up to that point she had been a darling of the movies, a child admired and enjoyed by audiences, a fact not for one minute lost on the people who employed her. *Miracle*, however, was the film that put her over the top.

No child had been more convincing: first as the great disbeliever in Santa Claus, then as a believer. There is a quality of truthfulness, of bone honesty to the performance that strikes me every time I see it. It wasn't until I was nearly grown myself that I realized that every time I saw the film I concentrated on her eyes. Not her face, not her movement, nothing but her eyes. Natalie acted with her eyes, and she did so as no other child actor had before her or has since.

Up until then she had been aware only that what she did, and what she was asked to do, gave certain people a great deal of pleasure. Mom particularly reacted with pleasure and approval. Men, too, tended to enforce her sense of well-being, especially those who directed her. George Seaton once said that Natalie acted with her heart, but that everything came out through her eyes, and I think at that time— when he directed *Miracle*—he was absolutely right. It was Irving Pichel, more than George, who encouraged her to run uninhibited, to bring to bear on each part all of the enthusiasm and spontaneity she had as a child.

That, tó me, was her secret. She was open, friendly, eager to please, a youthful tabula rasa upon which first her directors, and then her fans, wrote their own fantasies. She was everybody's ideal as a child, the successor to Shirley Temple and Elizabeth Taylor. It was a role for which she was ideally suited, and it was one she played—without ever really knowing it—perfectly. "It was what I did," she said to me once, "and it never occurred to me to do otherwise. I gave pleasure and that, in turn, pleased me."

She could also transform a living monster of a child into an adorable brat. It was in *Dear Brat*, I think, that the poor beleaguered television repairman was subjected to her tomboyish behavior. He was working away as she clattered in and out on her roller skates, her bottle-cap collection securely fastened onto her beanie. She asked irritating and marginally obnoxious questions and made a thorough pest of herself. She did it and she was adorable. The television repairman finally gave up and suggested she go play in traffic and that on her way out to getting run over she have a mouthful of razor blades to chew. Something to that effect, anyway, because my memory is not of what he said but of the fact that Natalie got away with it.

All of that changed with *Rebel Without a Cause*. It joined *Miracle* on the list of cult films, films which had a social impact well beyond their imagined story and characters. In it she played an adult, a disturbed, alienated, angry young woman who, in her way, was as much a rebel as James Dean.

Gone was the uninhibited little girl and in her place was the guarded, reserved young woman. It was a part which paralleled her life more closely than even she wanted to admit. By the time she began making the film—she was not quite sixteen—she too had begun to question things, to sense the unsteady ground on which any actresses' career is based. She was getting nervous, she was learning to make demands—both on herself and on those around her. She had begun to understand power and to use it, something she told me she began to understand at about the same time she began to discover just how insecure she really was, and how ephemeral her success could be if she didn't work hard at it.

For years she went from film to film, sometimes as many as four a year. By 1954, when *Rebel* was shot, she was averaging two a year, and with the exception of *The Searchers* in 1955, in which she did not appear for most of the film, it wasn't until *Marjorie Morningstar* in 1957 that she really turned in a major performance. In that film she was a Jewish princess falling in love with a man and with the theater, kicking over the traces of her past and trying to move forward. If you substitute "film" for "theater," you have a description of Natalie at that point in her life. The man was R.J., the past was her family, and the future was what concerned her.

Splendor in the Grass convinced Natalie—and many others—of one important thing. She had been a child star and now she was an adult star. Her character, clinging precariously to her virginity in the face of an assault by the character played by Warren Beatty, was, Natalie said in the years to come, a real bit of acting. She herself was no longer repressed, no longer a young lady. She was a woman, and she was beginning to like it. In the film itself she finally goes insane. In her life, she fell for Warren. It was, in many respects, a watershed film for her and years later she named her boat *Splendour*, after the film—an irony, since by that time she and R.J. were back together and had both recovered from the film and the events which had driven them apart years before. Natalie's concession to all of that was to stick the "u" into the boat's name to keep everything one step removed from the film itself. "It's the movie where I began to find myself," she told me, and in that she was exactly right. Years later she would find herself again by spending weekends on the *Splendour*.

West Side Story in 1961 was a success, but Natalie's portrayal of Maria, the beautiful young Puerto Rican girl, was not—and Natalie had sensed trouble ahead even before filming began. "I wanted the challenge," she explained later. Then came *Gypsy*, in which her singing voice was dubbed, but in which there is no mistaking her appeal and her beauty.

What had happened by now was that Natalie had made the transition from being everybody's favorite child to being an idealized young woman. There was something insouciantly accessible about her, something both vulnerable and trusting. She was the sort of woman men wanted, while at the same time women liked. She knew this, though she could never understand why it was. Those dual appeals, to both men and women, got her nominated for her third Academy Award for *Love with the Proper Stranger*. It was, basically, a love story, but it also confronted an issue very much on the minds of young men and women of the time: pregnancy. Abortions were still illegal and dangerous, and if the film seems a bit dated in subject now, it is timeless in its basic appeal: love. Steve McQueen was perfectly cast, rough at the edges yet tender in the center. Natalie was never lovelier. It is among my favorites of her films.

Love with the Proper Stranger was released in 1963, and though she went on to make *Sex and the Single Girl* and *The Great Race* immediately afterward, neither film was important in terms of her career. Then she made *Inside Daisy Clover* and began what she later called her hot streak.

In it, Daisy in one sense parallels Natalie. She is a poor girl from nowhere who, in this instance, makes a record and becomes a star. She marries her blond dream, played by Robert Redford, discovers he is homosexual, then proceeds to try to hold together both a faltering career and professional life. In the end, she is turning on the gas jets in her beachhouse and we are meant to believe that she may be going to commit suicide. Instead, she blows up her whole expensive beachhouse, that symbol of her success, her career, her glamorous life, and walks away from it all, taking only her coffee cup with her. It was something Natalie wanted to do on any number of occasions, but she always opted to stay, to remain a star, to fight the good fight. It was all she really knew how to do.

The hot streak went directly on to *This Property Is Condemned*, a film remarkable for its slim plot and strong performances—again Natalie and Robert Redford, this time directed by Sidney Pollack. The appeal was watching two beautiful people become lovers on screen, and there were no two better suited to such an enterprise.

From 1966, when *This Property Is Condemned* was released, until she made *Bob & Carol & Ted & Alice* in 1968, she made only one film, *Penelope*, which was a failure.

The Natalie of *Bob & Carol & Ted & Alice* was another new woman. This time it was Natalie as a mother and an adult. This time it was Natalie valiantly attempting comedy, something she wasn't comfortable with. This time it was Natalie poking fun at sexual mores, something she did enjoy doing. This time it was Natalie playing a Beverly Hills housewife. It was typecasting. Its success was largely unexpected —at least by Natalie—and all that happened delighted her, gave her a new optimism for her career. It would, she believed, go on forever.

And it might have, but we will never know. There were only five more films. She virtually dropped in for a day's work on *The Candidate*, then put her all into a film called *Peeper*, co-starring Michael Caine. It was an immediate flop, and was rereleased a year later as *Fat Chance*, flopping again. Then she made *Meteor*, *The Last Married Couple in America*, and *Brainstorm*.

By the time she made *Meteor*, her insecurities about the future had begun to influence her otherwise professional behavior on the set. *Meteor*, she once said, was about nothing more than getting work for several big names, among them Sean Connery, Karl Malden, and Henry Fonda. Ronald Neame, an Englishman with a courtly, lovely manner, was the director. He was a man it was impossible to dislike and easy to trust—that was, and is, his reputation. Natalie plunged in eagerly and enjoyed it all until the day Mr. Neame sent word around that she was wearing too much makeup, and would she take a bit of it off. Natalie balked. Negotiations took place and the final agreement was that Natalie would take off a bit of eye makeup, but not a whole lot more. That didn't work, so Mr. Neame asked for a bit more to come off.

Specifically, he wanted less mascara on her eyes and wanted it replaced by a light powder.

"Tell him I'd be happy to wear less makeup," she announced. "But only if Sean will work without his toupee."

She began to shift her emphasis to television. She did *Cat on a Hot Tin Roof* with R.J. and Laurence Olivier in 1976. The reviews were scathing, but the ratings were good. She was pleased with her work in *From Here to Eternity* in 1979, and furious when *The Memory of Eva Ryker* was bumped out of prime time in 1980. It was a role she relished, though doing the part where her character drowns on the *Titanic* had revived all of her old fears about the water.

She loved making movies—they were her life, a life from which her children rescued her briefly, but one to which she returned by choice. There were conditions to the resumption of her career after her children were born. She would not make any film which required her to go on location for any extended period. She would not, she said, be an absentee mother or wife.

Natalie was old Hollywood, but she was not old. She was the creation of the studio system, a system which ceased to exist in her lifetime. She was taught to be dependent upon that system, and when it expired she taught herself to be independent. She was not a natural actress, not a great talent, and she made a number of bad pictures. But she was a star, and she lived up to what was expected of her. She had her shining moments, and she had the courage to stretch herself to the limits of her talent.

There was not another hot streak, and the time between films had begun to lengthen. What would have happened had she lived? I have my own scenario. It has a happy ending. Natalie would be a success on stage—not a great one, but it would be a career which would give her the promise of work whenever she wanted it. She would begin to play the occasional character role and would do it so well that, before she was fifty, she would have her Academy Award. She would continue to be a pillar of her community. She would not become the sort of caricature of stardom that Elizabeth Taylor became. Nobody ages gracefully, but Natalie would have. She made it from child to adult to wife and mother with the whole world watching, and she would have made it to grandmother, too.

26

While I was making—literally if not figuratively—a splash in *Diamonds Are Forever*, Natalie was doing an unbilled cameo for Robert Redford in *The Candidate*, playing herself. She looked beautiful and she was desperately unhappy. Her marriage had ended badly, she found few men who interested her. She had an infant child to look after, and a career which was going nowhere.

The years in between films she dutifully went to her analyst, frequently had friends over, dated a bit, and read scripts. She rid herself of most of the people who had been making her career decisions in recent years. Natalie was in a period of flux and change—and worry.

"You know what it is," she said, putting down her fork and staring forlornly at the sliced tomatoes and the small piece of cold chicken her diet allowed her for lunch. "It's an addiction. There's this hook. Not the one they use to pull you off stage in vaudeville. The other kind of hook. You get a part, you make money. The hook is that you believe you'll always get another part and always get more money. Jesus, sometimes I hate this business."

"Me too," I muttered, though at the moment it wasn't exactly the truth as far as I was concerned. I was in demand, a situation which did not add a great deal to our relationship. As soon as I was finished with *Diamonds Are Forever*, I was offered the starring role in an independent film, *A Place Called Today*. I played a journalist—one who, I might add, kept her clothes on except for one brief scene, and was required to act—investigating some political evildoings. It was a film which had serious intentions, and as soon as I read the script I agreed to do it. My agent stopped me short by saying, "Shouldn't we ask what they're paying?"

"If you have to, then ask. And then say yes," I ordered.

How independent was it? So independent that I was the only "name star." It was so independent they considered me both a name and a star. I figured I was good for selling about ten tickets—maybe twenty, now that *Playboy* had taken my pictures. The film was shot in New Jersey and we all lived in a nearby hotel. For trips to New York on the weekend, there were no limousines, no perks at all. We went to the train station and bought our own tickets at our own expense. It was a world apart from the big-budget doings of James Bond, a film whose pretenses were all in its script, and everything else was secondary. We even had rehearsal time. I adored every minute of it. For the first time in my life I was beginning to feel I was actually an actress.

My leading man was from Texas and the only film he had ever made had been his screen test for this picture. Richard Smedley was extremely handsome, extremely intense, full of rough edges, and completely lacking in sophistication. He was perfect for the part of the journalist who joins me in my quest. Both he and I were to be murdered at the end of the picture, shot down as we reached out for one another. It was to be that kind of picture. Because he was inexperienced and insecure, he was at first difficult to work with. During one rehearsal I quietly whispered a suggestion to him. He took it as a personal criticism and wrote me a note telling me what to do with myself "and the spotted pony you rode in on." I was thoroughly puzzled because I'd never heard that expression before.

One night he appeared at my door with a bottle of wine he'd bought for the two of us. I was engrossed in a book and had moved into a small world of my own and was reluctant to leave it. But his invitation had an edge of need to it, and I agreed. We drank the wine and he told me about himself. He was from a big, loving family, one that was spread all over Texas and very close. He had no money, just a desire to be an actor, and was the first in his family to leave Texas. It was obvious to me he was lonely and frightened, but just as obvious he was determined and ambitious.

Occasionally, on those weekends we didn't shoot

on Saturdays, I'd take the train into New York. Michael had a suite I used, and once Michael was there and we went out on the town. The great romance was over, but it was hard for both of us to let go. The truth is that there were occasional slips in our determination to be friends only, but I know of no slips that gave as much pleasure as ours did. Slips or not, my focus was now primarily elsewhere, and at the end of the few weekends I spent in New York, I was back on the grimy train to New Jersey and *A Place Called Today.*

Richard Smedley was everything I was unaccustomed to. I did not even consider the possibility of a romance until once again he materialized with a bottle of wine. As we drank it he confessed that he was lonely and missed being surrounded by his family, and that he was uncertain about his future as an actor. I told him uncertainty was one of the conditions of acting, which I hoped made him feel better. He was endearingly hangdog and most appealing. Finally he asked if he could spend the night and I said no.

He persisted. He said he was lonely and that if I'd let him, he'd spend the night. He promised not to touch me. And that is exactly what happened. From then on we were together. Now when I went into New York it was with Richard. Dinner wasn't at La Grenouille, it was at whatever place we happened to find when we got hungry. There were no big apartments, just small hotel rooms. When he finally wore down my resistance, I was already half in love and we became lovers who were all but inseparable. There was nothing phony about Richard: what you saw was what you got. I was smitten with his lack of pretense.

I telephoned Natalie and told her everything. I chattered on and Natalie listened, and it was not until I was far into my story that I realized Natalie's silences were comments too. Finally she spoke.

"I think you're being impulsive."

I had to agree. I had been impulsive all my life. But I was never certain of the difference between impulse and instinct. My instinct about Richard was good. I said so. "I'm also in love," I added. "For the first time. Truly in love."

"What about Michael? Wasn't that love?"

"Yes, but there was no future to it. You said so yourself."

"Well, I hope you do better this time than the other times."

Nothing like a little optimism to keep things going. I put down the phone and sat in my room for some time, thinking things over, trying to decide whether I was making the right decision. Every relationship I had ever had with a man had ended in disaster, with the sole exception of Michael, and even that hadn't yielded what I had hoped for. Was Natalie right? Was I being impulsive and making a big mistake? I didn't think so.

The only cloud on our horizon was what to do when the picture was finished. Richard intended to return to Texas and wait to see what happened with the picture before pursuing his career. I was going back to Los Angeles. I had already agreed to start work on another picture, so Texas was out of the question for me. I finally persuaded Richard to come back to Los Angeles with me, and he agreed, on one condition: that we be married. I told him my record at marriage was a sorry one, and one by one I ticked off my failures. He asked if I still believed in marriage, and I said yes.

"Well, then?"

I kept putting him off and he kept insisting. Richard won, and by that time I was as in love with the idea of marriage as I was in love with Richard. I had even decided that I wanted to have children. We went to Los Angeles as soon as the picture wrapped and I immediately took Richard to meet my famous older sister, as he jokingly called her. Natalie was wary about Richard, worried our love would not last. It was a time in her life when she was suspicious of all relationships. Nevertheless, she decided she would put on our wedding for us. My actual experience with the marriage ceremony itself had been with Tijuana quickies, Las Vegas quickies, and L.A. judges, and it was time, Natalie said, that I have a proper marriage ceremony.

There were flowers and friends all over Natalie's house the day I married Richard, and it was one of the happiest days of my life. My family was united once again, my rift with Natalie had ended, my career was going great guns, and my life with Richard lay ahead. My one wish was for Natalie. I wanted her to be in love too, to be married and to be as happy as I

was. I told her that day what I wanted for her, and we
held one another and cried.

"I need more than that," she cried, wiping away
her tears and smiling bravely. "I need a couple of
good pictures, too."

27

We didn't have much money, but we had each other. We rented a small house off Doheny, not far from the Sunset Strip. It had no air-conditioning, just one small floor heater, and it needed a new kitchen floor, which Richard and I put in ourselves. I made the curtains and pillow covers. It was very different from the high life I had become accustomed to, but I loved it. I also went from audition to audition and ended up doing quite a lot of television, from three episodes of *Police Story* to *Baretta*.

After I had posed for *Playboy* and done the Bond film, it became something of a joke among my friends to say I'd never do a Disney film. I was considered not-quite-Disney material. Jack Gilardi, my agent, was not without a sense of humor when it came to the sort of roles available to me. "If you're the girl next door, Lana, then you live in a pretty racy neighborhood," Jack said. Imagine my surprise when I was summoned to Disney to audition for *Justin Morgan Had a Horse*. Imagine my surprise when I got the part! I made sure they understood I had appeared in *Play-*

boy in not much and in *Diamonds Are Forever* in less, and they seemed to think that might work to their advantage. Times had changed.

I played an indentured Irish servant girl who falls in love with Don Murray, who, in turn, has to raise the money to buy me away from the evil Squire Fisk, all the while trying to raise a Morgan horse. Heavy stuff, and I enjoyed every minute of it. The film was shot entirely on the Disney ranch during the hottest months of summer. There were dogs as well as horses in the picture, and while the horses were well cared for, I was not happy watching the dogs being locked into cages when they were not being used. One day they were yelping in protest when I wandered by, so I let them all loose. The trainer was furious, and I was as innocent-looking as I could be, though I suspect he knew I did it because I'd been complaining about the cages—which were perfectly legal—for several days.

Meanwhile, *A Place Called Today*, our serious independent film, was ready for release, and full of high hopes, Richard and I went to a screening of it. It was dreadful. Late-night television is full of turkeys that were made with the best of intentions, and this bomb is one of them. Richard, in particular, came off as though he was being punished for some imaginary crime. I can't imagine why they chose the cuts they did. We had all seen the rushes and there were plenty of takes where Richard's lack of experience was replaced by an emerging—and good—young actor. He slid deeper and deeper into the seat beside me.

It couldn't have happened at a worse time for him. He'd summoned his courage to make the move to Los Angeles, and then he'd begun making the rounds of the casting agents. To one and all he said to go see his film when it came out. It was to be his calling card, and it was going to lead him to work in television and films. It was to be the beginning of his successful career. We both believed that.

The image persists that a working actor makes a great deal of money. It isn't necessarily so. Because I had experience and two series (one very successful) in my past, I was paid more than most actresses. But. The jobs were sometimes months apart and I was supporting two of us—and doing it, I thought, while giving the impression that Richard's potential made all the discomfort of a wife being the breadwinner worthwhile. Now that we'd seen *A Place Called Today*, we both began to worry about tomorrow.

A friend had been after Richard to take a job in his public relations firm, and Richard had resisted. As his chances for an acting career diminished, Richard reconsidered. It was, I told him, something he would be very good at. He was smart, good-looking, and at heart a businessman as much as an actor. So my husband became a P.R. man while I continued going from television show to television show, taking great care not to talk about my work when I was at home. It was an awkward time for us both, but I think we made the best of it. It was a strain on our marriage, one that we both carefully covered up, and so it did not show for several more years, and by then it was too late.

I saw Natalie often, though usually without Richard. I was working, married and settled; Natalie was working only occasionally, lonely and unsettled, still bitter over her divorce. She frequently seemed distracted, but she made it clear that her need was for her daughter and for her family, and so we often went to lunch together. She would ask after Richard, I'd respond, and then I'd ask about Natasha and Natalie would be off. Other times she'd bring up her work, make some crack about finding good parts, or she'd remark that she'd been out with so-and-so who had turned out to be a dud. I have few memories of who she dated during this time because she seldom dated anyone more than twice and they tended not to be actors or anyone famous. Rich, maybe, but not famous.

It was a difficult time for Mom and Pop, too. Natalie was keeping Mom at arm's length and not letting her spend much time with Natasha. Pop, who had had a series of minor heart attacks, finally had a big one. For a while neither Natalie nor I reacted much—it was, by now, a case of crying wolf too often. But we did react when he was rushed to the hospital for a pacemaker. Mom reacted too. She went into hysterics and then collapsed. She was rushed to another hospital. As soon as Mom could be moved, we had her taken to the same hospital Pop was in, simplifying things somewhat for Natalie and me. Pop had also had a heart attack when Natalie was pregnant with Natasha, and when I had called her to ask her to come to the hospital with me, Natalie refused. She was afraid of losing her baby, afraid the tension and the excitement would be too much. I was annoyed, but I understood, too. This time, however, Natalie plunged in and we both took turns going from floor to floor, cheering up Pop and trying not to be irritated with Mom. She has one reaction to pressure of this sort: collapse.

Richard was wonderful. He was always there when I needed him, always eager to help.

"Boy, did you get lucky," Natalie whispered to me one night after Richard had done half a dozen errands—hers and mine. Pop—and Mom—recovered.

It seems as I look back on those days that there were only short periods of calm between bursts of excitement. The next thing that happened began without any of us knowing anything about it and soon became the talk of the town. The first I knew of it was when Richard and I arrived for dinner at Natalie's. Mom and Pop were there too. To say we were shocked to be greeted at the door by Natalie with her arm linked to a beaming Robert Wagner is to make a gross understatement. It was such a surprise that Mom was speechless.

"Surprise!" Natalie said as we walked in. "There are happy endings after all."

We were all full of questions, and Natalie obligingly answered them all. Their reconciliation had begun over a year before. Quietly, without—they insisted—either of them really knowing it was happening. There was a peace to be made first, the sort of peace which comes with finally putting an unhappy memory into the past and leaving it there. It began at a dinner party. By that time R.J. was divorced and Natalie was temporarily without Richard, who had gone off to London on business. Linda and John Foreman had a dinner party and invited both Natalie and R.J., but not before inquiring if such an arrangement would make either of them uncomfortable. Both insisted it would not and Natalie said that was how it worked out. They resumed nothing more than a friendship that night, but for the first time in years they did sit down and talk. Linda Foreman later told me it was a long talk, with the two of them sitting in a corner, Natalie leaning forward, her elbows on her knees, her chin resting on her hands. Linda claimed she believed then something was about to happen.

Nothing did. Instead, they both went their separate ways. Then, when Natalie had put Richard Gregson out of her life for good, R.J. waited awhile and then he called.

"I was afraid to call at first because I thought she'd refuse to see me," R.J. told us.

Thereafter things happened fast. They fell as hard as, if not harder than, they had the first time. They were thrilled and confused and they kept it a secret. They hadn't so much as gone to a restaurant together. It happened quickly, in only a few weeks, and by the evening Natalie gathered us all together to tell us, they not only announced they were back together, they told us they would be getting married as soon as possible.

While we were all recovering from our shock, Natalie hurried into the kitchen to get some more champagne and I rushed in right behind her.

"I can't believe it!"

"Neither can I. What do you think? Do you think we're crazy?"

"No. I see a happy woman. That's all I need to know."

We hugged and kissed, and both of us were crying. We all sat down to dinner in Natalie's elegant dining room, with its crystal chandelier, and toasted them with champagne poured into her best Baccarat glasses. Natasha, still a baby, gurgled and ate with her hands. She too got a sip of champagne.

That night was quite a celebration.

28

The news began to spread, but it took several more weeks before Natalie and R.J. made it public. When they did, they caused a sensation. I once asked Natalie if it had all been carefully planned, and she said no, but there was no mistaking the twinkle in her eyes. On the movies' most glamorous night of the year, Natalie and R.J. showed up together—the night of the Academy Awards in 1972. A limousine pulled up to the theater and out stepped Natalie and R.J. The photographers started a rampage, and so did the fans in the bleachers. It was a reunion the whole world felt sentimental about. Their appearance was mentioned in virtually every story written about that night, and their pictures were on every television screen in the country.

Their remarriage in July was as rigorously private as their reappearance together had been public. They chartered a boat, rounded up their close friends, families, their respective daughters, and in a burst of good humor had "The Second Time Around" printed on all the napkins and matchbooks for the wedding. It was late afternoon by the time everybody was on board, and we set sail immediately. The boat cruised out through the breakwater and into the rolling Pacific, and up the coast a bit until it came to a stop just off the Malibu coastline. Natalie and R.J. were at sea, where they'd loved to be the first time around, and now, at sunset, with a judge performing the ceremony, they were re-wed. There was hardly a dry eye among us. I, for one, wept. John Lindon, Natalie's psychoanalyst for all those many years, went from one guest to another and recorded everybody's congratulations on his tape recorder. Richard, who was a very good photographer, was asked by Natalie to take all the pictures. He was flattered to be asked and shot rolls and rolls of film.

"There's only one moment that will go unrecorded," he joked to R.J.

"It's already happened." R.J. laughed. Natalie heard and gave him a playful poke in the ribs.

I know that brides are always described as radiant, but I can only say that watching her get married in a beautiful Pacific sunset, and knowing all that had preceded this moment, Natalie gave radiance a new dimension. She wore a long gingham cotton dress trimmed with lace. Her sleeves were short and puffed, and in each square of violet gingham were tiny rosebuds. She wore her hair long and loose. R.J. beamed the whole time.

After the marriage and the champagne—of which there was a great deal—the boat returned to port and everybody except Natalie and R.J. got off. We all stood on shore and waved as they set sail immediately. They spent several days sailing up and down the coast and over to Catalina. It was a voyage they had made many times before and would make many times again.

Richard had promised Natalie and R.J. he'd have the photographs all printed up and ready by the time they got back. Early the next morning, he went to the laboratory to supervise the developing and printing. When he came home later in the day we spent several hours looking at the pictures. I liked them. They were good and they had been shot by my husband and so I hoped they would mean even more to Natalie. We called Mom and Pop and they came over and looked at them too.

The next morning Mom called and said a friend of hers, a lady named Marcia Borie, had telephoned. Marcia had been at Natalie and R.J.'s first wedding and now had connections at several fan magazines. Since Richard had the only photographs of the wedding, Mom would arrange for her friend to pay him several hundred dollars for copies.

"You sure it's all right?" I asked her. Natalie had not said anything about the pictures themselves, she had just asked Richard to take them. There had been no prohibitions spoken or understood. Still, I felt a slight reluctance about selling them. Richard was delighted with the idea of published photos—with a credit, of course—and payment too. Both Richard and Mom dismissed my slight misgivings, and so, finally, did I. The pictures were delivered to Mom's friend and that was that. The next time any of us gave it any thought at all was when the check arrived and Richard called Mom to thank her.

If what follows sounds like some sort of convoluted Russian novel, that's because it is exactly what it seemed like to Richard and me. We heard no more about the pictures we sold to the magazine. Natalie and R.J., meanwhile, had come home from their honeymoon, had seen the pictures, and were delighted with them. I went to their house for dinner a couple of times, and Katie Wagner, R.J.'s daughter, began dropping in at our apartment from time to time because there were lots of kids around. It was all very familylike and very friendly. Then the pictures were published.

Natalie and R.J. were enraged. The first we heard of it was from Mom, who called—her voice shaking— to tell us Natalie and R.J. had seen the pictures. They considered Richard's selling them a gross and thoughtless invasion of their privacy. Mom stressed Richard's name, but it was obvious I was implicated too, and so I asked if they were angry at me as well.

"Yes," Mom said.

"How about you?" I asked her. After all, she had made all the arrangements.

"They don't know. Please, Lana, do not make trouble for me." She was crying.

I immediately called Natalie to apologize, to do anything at all to make peace. She refused my call. I waited a few hours and called again. Nothing. Richard called R.J., and the response was the same. I wanted desperately to explain and defend myself and Richard, but I also felt I had to remain loyal to Mom. I never did tell Natalie what happened. Ever.

I telephoned Mom and asked her to intervene and make peace. The idea that Richard and I had somehow ruined Natalie and R.J.'s memory of that moment by selling the pictures made me sick at heart. Mom suggested we let time heal the wounds. Mom had much to lose, and I think it's typical of all of our tangled relationships that I felt obliged to protect her at this point, to spare her Natalie's wrath.

I looked at the pictures again. They were lovely. Natalie and R.J. looked dazzling. Then I looked at the pictures as they had been reproduced in the fan magazine. They were no different. I sat down and wrote Natalie a letter, taking care to make no defense of what Richard and I had done and particular care not to mention Mom's participation. I apologized profusely.

There was no answer. I telephoned Mom again and asked for her help. She said she believed Natalie and R.J. were both overreacting, but said there was nothing she could do. Not now, anyway. She, of course, was desperately afraid of incurring Natalie's anger too, and I understood her fear. Somehow the fact that Richard and I were taking the blame for something that was partially her fault as well seemed perfectly natural.

It was well over a year before I spoke to or saw Natalie again.

29

I kept working, never steadily, but frequently enough to supplement Richard's income. For one who was accustomed to living as I had for so many years, the settled nature of marriage was something I loved. The fact that we didn't have much money didn't bother me at all. Richard experimented with various businesses, sometimes successfully, sometimes not, but always looking for something at which he'd succeed. It was only a matter of time, we were certain of it. He was a resilient man, one who accepted the disappointment of his career as an actor, then got on with his life. From time to time we'd go to Texas, and I adored his family, their sense of togetherness and their openness with one another. I was not at all like the other women in his family and I sensed some unfriendliness toward me, but most were kind. It was quite a new experience for me.

The fact that I had a successful marriage made up for the other great void in my life. It was, of course, easy to keep track of Natalie and R.J. Their names were constantly in the social columns, attending this party, that premiere, or entertaining on their own. Then they moved to R.J.'s house in Palm Springs. I heard of them also from Mom, who reported on visits with them. Once I spotted their picture in the paper. They were standing together, drinks in hand, elegantly dressed at a party. I blinked back my tears. Why, I wondered over and over, had I placed so much importance on our relationship, why was it I so wanted Natalie's approbation and love?

Finally I went to a psychiatrist. I didn't so much feel any special need for help, I rather felt a need for an impartial audience. Richard, of course, was staunchly on my side, and while I accepted our banishment with quiet resignation, he was open in his anger, both at Mom for not admitting her participation and at Natalie and R.J. for the estrangement. By now he believed selling the pictures had been the wrong thing to do. We had discussed Natalie's anger over the photographers at her high-school graduation, both Natalie's and R.J.'s anger at R.J.'s friend who sold pictures of them on their first honeymoon.

The psychiatrist listened for several weeks and then said I was so desperate for my sister's love and approval that I'd accept anything she said to me, even that I was guilty of destroying their privacy. A much-sought privacy, he pointed out, wanted so very much that they turned up together at the Academy Awards and stopped for every single photographer there. They had since lived their life very much in the limelight, had given interviews, and clearly nourished the publicity.

"Their wedding is different," I cried.

"Not all that much," he argued. He contended I should get angry right back and confront Natalie. That, I simply couldn't do.

"Fuck 'em all," Richard said.

"And the spotted pony they rode in on," I added, but not with much conviction.

Richard now traveled from time to time, and when he was gone, I stayed at home alone. Once or twice Mom came by to stay with me, but my company was pretty much limited to my pets. Richard and I had friends of our own, but we tended to see them when we were together. My friends, people Richard referred to as "from the old days," I seldom if ever saw. They lived the old life, the one I'd left. Bob Bell, whom I had first met when he was my neighbor at Shoreham Towers when I was working on *Peyton Place*, remained the only friend "from the old days," just as he is a friend today. He has survived the true test of friendship, which is to say he has tolerated practical jokes and enough antics to strain the patience of the most patient of friends.

I worked from time to time, whenever parts came along, but once again I did not actively pursue my career. I did not go to parties, I was not seen out and about town, nor did I do any of the other things an actress was expected to do in a business where visibility is all.

Life, as they say, went on. I never got used to the fact that my sister did not want me in her life, but I finally accepted it. Natalie and R.J. made a television movie together called *The Affair*, which was essentially a love story. I had seen Natalie's movies on television from time to time, but with the exception of *The Candidate*, she hadn't made any new pictures, so about the only place I saw her was late at night on television. I watched *The Affair* with tears in my eyes. She was positively beautiful, and in it she did something that sent me hurtling back over the years to another time and another marriage. In the course of the story she had a confrontation with R.J.'s character, and in it she was holding a wineglass. She broke the glass and cut her hand—just as she had done the day she arrived at the house to tell us that she and R.J. had separated, an eerie irony. I wanted to write and tell her how well she had done, but I could not tolerate the thought that my attempt at congratulation might be rejected, and so I did nothing.

In the fall of that same year, 1973, Mom called to tell me that Natalie was pregnant. I conveyed my congratulations to her through Mom, but I no longer asked Mom to bring us back together. She would do nothing that might risk Natalie's or R.J.'s displeasure, and I wasn't about to ask her something she would refuse to do. I realized that for the first time in years I was actually envious of Natalie. Here we were, scraping to make ends meet, and there was Natalie, pregnant, with her beautiful home and her servants, leading the charmed life.

Now I watched the newspapers more carefully, looking to see how Natalie looked as the pregnancy progressed. She and R.J. appeared at some function, some salute—I forget what it was, except that it was one of the movies' many self-congratulatory occasions—and there was Natalie, obviously pregnant, her cheeks filling out along with her stomach. Natalie had gone through adolescence without once looking bad, without once stretching out in the wrong direction at the wrong time, and now she was going through her second pregnancy with all of the style and beauty characteristic of her whole life.

Then, wonder of wonders, five months later I turned up pregnant too. Richard and I were delirious with joy. I thought too that this might give me something in common with Natalie, some new ground on which to reestablish our friendship. I thought in vain. Because I am small and quite slender, it was no time at all until I was too pregnant to work any longer. Richard and I really went on a budget, determined to make ends meet on his salary. For the first—and so far only—time in my life I successfully managed to pinch pennies. I was so organized that I didn't even go to the laundromat until I had enough for two jam-packed loads, because I'd discovered that two big loads of wash could be crammed into one dryer. As Richard put it, he got used to being without underwear on the weekends and was starting to like it.

Natalie and R.J. frequently came to town from Palm Springs, and I read of baby showers and parties, or heard about them from Mom. My friends gave me a shower, too, and in the middle of it I excused myself and went to the bathroom and cried. I missed Natalie terribly. I tried to tell Richard how it felt to have someone who had always been an essential part of your life taken away from you, but not really taken away because she was there to be seen and read about. He sympathized, but I know if I asked him today he'd still be angry with Natalie and R.J., sorry about the pictures, but, as he said once in a moment of anger: "Christ, you'd think I'd killed their firstborn."

30

Finally I wrote to her. It was a short note composed over and over and what it said was that now that I was having a child, I hoped that child would be able to know its cousins. And I hoped it was possible for Natalie and me to once again be friends and sisters. That, I stressed, was the most important thing of all. She was, I wrote, such an important part of my life that I hoped she would be a part of my child's life too. I wanted my family to be complete.

A little more than a week later, she wrote back. I stood in the kitchen and looked at the letter several minutes before opening it. It began by saying how delighted she was that I was having a child, and then went on to say that she was sorry but she simply did not have time for the friendship I was requesting. However—and it became a word that stuck in my mind for months afterward—if I was willing to go to a psychoanalyst, she would be more than willing to pay for my analysis.

I started weeping. Then I started screaming. Several hours later, when I finally had some semblance of control of myself, I sat down and wrote her a letter. I told her I'd seen a psychiatrist, that I didn't feel I needed help. I said I knew I'd screwed up a lot of my life, but I took full responsibility for it and felt fine about myself now. I simply wrote because I wanted to become friends again with the person who had been the most important to me in my life, more important than either our mother or father. I don't remember now what else I said. I know for sure I did not express the anger or the hurt I felt, only that I kept pleading.

I was just finishing the letter when Richard came home, and as I stammered out what had happened, I began weeping and screaming all over again. I finally grabbed the letter I had written, ran out of the house, and drove off to mail it. I was halfway down the block before Richard, in his car, caught up with me. He followed me, shouting for me to stop, and I kept on going. When I finally got to the mailbox, I pulled over and got out to mail my letter. Richard caught me just as I was about to drop the letter in the slot. He took it out of my hand, pulled me into his arms, and said he refused to let me answer it, would not let me be hurt anymore. He tore the letter in half and, with me sobbing, led me back to my car and followed me home.

It couldn't have just been the pictures; there had to be more. I wondered if R.J. just didn't want me around. I knew too that Mom was having some trouble with Natalie and was being made to keep her distance. Mom, of course, did exactly as Natalie wished. But then, I thought, I did too. There were no answers—and there never would be.

Richard was traveling more and more, and I spent the next months pretty much alone. He came home on the weekends, and for me those were my happiest times. I saw Mom fairly often, and from time to time she'd tell about visiting Natalie, but now she, too, was careful to avoid the subject. I no longer even considered asking her to intervene with Natalie. If anything was to be resolved, it would be resolved by Natalie only, and not by anyone else.

Then one day the phone rang and it was Mom:

"Natalie has come up from Palm Springs to be near her doctor. It's almost time. She would like you to come and have lunch with the two of us on Friday." It was also my birthday, a fact not mentioned at the time.

I didn't say, "Tell Natalie to go to hell." I didn't say, "Why can't she call herself?" I didn't say, "Not until we discuss a few things." What I said was: "What time and where?"

I had seen a pattern for a diaper bag in one of the women's magazines and had ripped it out, thinking I'd love to make one for Natalie and one for myself. But each time I looked at the pattern, I thought of all that was going on and did nothing with it. Now I flew into action. I had five days, and if I really got busy, I figured I could get it done.

It was a diaper bag made out of a pair of cut-up Levi's, with gingham sewn over the pockets and sewn inside as a lining. The shoulder strap was a strip of the pants embroidered by hand. I got it all done by myself except for the zipper. I took that to a tailor. Considering I had not been exactly the domestic type most of my life, I thought my diaper bag was a triumph. I wanted to give Natalie something original, something special, and this was it. Many years later, I discovered she had thrown it away upon arriving home.

The day of the lunch I was half-tempted to drop the diaper bag at the hotel and run. I felt no matter what I did it probably wouldn't be right. But I also wanted to see Natalie so much that I walked into the Beverly Wilshire Hotel, rang her room, and went up. Mom opened the door. The first thing either of us did was giggle. There was Natalie, tiny as ever, hugely pregnant, and even though I was five months behind her, I was already as big as the side of a barn. Natalie had cut her hair short and gaminelike, and was wearing a loose Mexican dress, all hand-embroidered. I wore a wool dress I had made for myself, and my strongest memory of it is that it always itched. We kissed one another on the cheek and Mom looked on, wringing her hands and looking incredibly pleased.

We ordered lunch and then exchanged presents. Natalie enthused over her diaper bag and seemed impressed I had made it myself. I enthused over the lovely blanket she had given me. When it came time for idle chatter, there was none. There was so very much that was not being said that it seemed to interfere with what little we did say. I would describe the lunch as strained but polite. Mom plunged in on several of the awkward silences, but not with much success. Finally she started talking about "Do you remember the time you girls . . . ?" and we all took refuge in the distant past.

Later that afternoon Mom called and said she felt everything had gone very well. I played my hunch—it was a pretty obvious one, at least to me.

"You talked her into it, didn't you?"

"Yes. I want you to be friends too. Natalie can be very stubborn."

"Why? Why all this time?"

"I asked her. She says she doesn't want to talk about it. So I never asked again."

That was as close as I've ever come to finding out what happened.

On March 9, 1974—just nine days after our lunch —Courtney Brooke Wagner was born, and Pop, who was hoping for one grandson at least to balance the load of females in his life, smiled and said, "Well, I should have known better." I told him I'd do my best to help him out.

"You do that, Lana," he said.

I went to a florist and picked out a bouquet full of fresh flowers on a stand of pretty stained-glass butterflies. The stand itself came off once the flowers had finished blooming and became one of those freestanding things you put in children's rooms to give them something colorful to look at.

Then I went to the hospital to see the baby and to congratulate Natalie. I was careful to keep the visit short, and I remember spending more time looking at Courtney—my curiosity about newborn babies was now as immense as I was—than I did talking to Natalie.

On August 11, just five months later, Evan Taylor Smedley was born. She had her father's round face and my coloring and she was, to me, the most impossibly beautiful little thing I'd ever seen. Richard was beside himself with excitement. I had never in the years I'd been with him seen him quite like this. Mom and Pop came immediately and stayed the whole twenty hours I was in labor before the doctors decided to perform a cesarean section.

"Sorry, Pop," I said as I kissed him on the cheek.

"I have beautiful daughters and beautiful granddaughters. Not so bad," he laughed.

It was several days before I heard from Natalie. First came flowers, followed by a beautiful silver baby-picture frame. Then, without any warning, Natalie herself arrived, kissed me and her baby niece, and enthusiastically endorsed the hospital for allowing me to keep Evan in the room with me. Then she was gone.

There was something new, very new in my life. For the first time I had someone I loved even more than I loved Natalie.

31

A child causes a major change in your life, and the many changes that accompanied the arrival of Evan were all welcome. She became the center of my small universe, the focus of my energies.

There had also been changes in my relationship with Richard but they were subtle and somewhat obscured by Evan's arrival. Richard had left public relations and was now a businessman dabbling in various undertakings, making a reasonable enough living, but he wanted more. Our lives were compartmentalized.

There was Richard's professional life, of which I was not a part. I'd ask from time to time, he'd begin an explanation of sorts, but I sensed he didn't really want to share it all with me. I had no particular objection and no reason to demand otherwise—I was from the sort of traditional family where the father went off and did his work and there wasn't much talk about it. Also, since I had no mind for business, I figured Richard was doing me a favor by not confusing me with details.

There was our life together. When Richard was due home from a trip, I had everything ready. The house was clean, his favorite food was in the refrigerator, everything was ready. We had an unspoken agreement about friends. Richard made the best of the fact that he hadn't succeeded as an actor, but he didn't want to be reminded of it. When I was working, I said little, and friends who were actors I saw when Richard was out of town. When he was at home, the people we saw were a collection of his friends and mutual friends.

And now there was Evan. She was the most incredibly watchful baby—she seemed to be watching everything. She was also a sunny, happy child. Evan was easy. We loved her dearly.

One day Mom and Pop were over and I had Evan on the changing table. Pop stood by me as I changed Evan's diaper. She was gurgling and wiggling, and I bent over and started kissing her tummy, holding her hands in mine and waving them about.

"You shouldn't do that, Lana," Pop said. "It'll give her all sorts of ideas."

"What sort of ideas?"

"You know what I mean," he replied. He was obviously uncomfortable and sorry he'd brought the subject up. I figured out what he was talking about by his discomfort.

"Oh, Pop. Don't be so silly."

"That's just what your sister says to me."

"She's right, Pop," I said, patting him on the arm. Pop had lived almost all of his life in America, but he was still very much from the old country and he still believed cuddling and kissing babies led them down the path to sexual trouble.

Through Mark Nathanson, one of my oldest friends, I was offered a part in a TV movie called *Little Ladies of the Night,* a story about teenagers working as prostitutes—and it sounded to me like a surefire ratings success. I accepted and, with Mom helping out, went back to work, sometimes taking Evan with me, sometimes leaving her at home. I wasn't looking for terrific parts from an acting standpoint—they are few and far between in television—I was after the most commercial projects I could get.

The success of the show brought me attention once again, attention Richard wasn't comfortable with. I understood how he felt and began the delicate juggling act of trying to draw attention to my work while not drawing attention to it whenever Richard was around.

"You've got to be seen. You've got to show up around town," my friend Mark insisted.

"I can't. I just can't." I didn't know what to do and so I did nothing.

Mom called and said Natalie would like me to bring Evan and come to Courtney's first birthday party. Once again the question was in the back of my mind, but it never came out of my mouth: Why didn't Natalie herself call? I was being invited—or summoned, if you prefer—and of course we went. The invitation did not include Richard, who had neither seen nor spoken to Natalie or R.J. since he took the last picture of them on their wedding day. The party was outdoors, and there were several other mothers there with infants. Natalie's greeting was warm, she held Evan and played with her for several minutes, and that was pretty much it. We all had lunch and then Evan and I went home.

"Did she invite us as a favor to you?" I asked Mom later.

"No. It was her idea," she answered.

Progress.

I went out on several interviews, and was even offered a part in a picture. I didn't like the script and didn't see much of a future for the picture and I declined it. Mark called and insisted I reconsider. I did and refused again.

Sometimes, when Richard was out of town I'd go to parties with Mark. I always told Richard I was going, and he never objected. The parties were part of being seen, and by now my life had become so centered on my marriage and Evan that I welcomed getting out from time to time. There is something interesting about a good Hollywood party: a worth-while one is filled with a lot of smart, hustling people who are working to get things done. It might be artificial, but it can be stimulating and—who knows? I didn't go often and I seldom stayed long, but I was getting out and around and thereby fulfilling one of the requirements of the business.

The relationship with Mark was one of friendship. It still is. Once, Mark called and wanted me to go to a dinner party with him, but Richard was home and naturally I couldn't. The unspoken agreement was that I'd be at home with Richard whenever he was there. I was astonished when Richard, who had overheard my conversation with Mark, insisted I go to the party without him. I said I'd go, but only if he'd come to. He refused, and ordered me to go. He himself called Mark back and said I'd go. I was in tears—of confusion, of indecision—but I got dressed and went.

I lived the next several months in two worlds. In one I was an actress, working occasionally, my reputation good. I went to a few industry gatherings to talk to producers and directors. In the other world I was a wife, staying at home with my husband and my infant daughter. There was a problem, though: Richard was traveling often, spending more and more time in his own world. We struggled against what was happening, attempted to make our lives right again, but the uncomfortable truth—one we were only beginning to face—was that our marriage was falling apart.

32

Richard's trips became longer and more mysterious. He would say he was going to Chicago, I'd ask what for, and he'd either change the subject or make some excuse for not telling me. Finally he yelled at me to mind my own business. I began to do just that. My rationalization was that Richard was feeling all kinds of pressures in his business life and I could help best by asking nothing at all.

Those times he was at home he was irritable and distant. If he came into the house and found me sitting with one of my girlfriends, he'd get furious. I was allowed no company, no friendships he did not approve. I think he allowed my friendship with Mark to continue only because he knew I needed that to survive—not in a financial sense, though that must have been a part of it, but in a psychological sense. I could move within certain bounds, and my only problem was figuring out just what the limits of those bounds were.

I didn't know what to do. I'd reached the point where I could no longer completely submerge myself in being a mother and a wife. For one thing, I was a wife who was now clearly relegated to a psychological oblivion. Evan was a year and a half old, walking, talking, a continual delight. But she was not enough and I felt then—and I still feel now—that I needed to work, to have some sort of job in addition to being a mother. Being a wife to an attentive and loving husband and father would have been job enough and it was one I was more than willing to fulfill. That, Richard was making it very clear, was not what he wanted. I began to believe Richard wanted out, and I was beginning to realize I did, too.

One night I was sitting in bed crying when I heard Richard come into the house, home from still another trip he had refused to say anything about. I heard him go into the kitchen and then he came to our bedroom. He saw that I was crying but did not ask what the matter was.

I asked for a divorce. I told him I was miserable, that the happiest years of my life had been when we were struggling, working together. It was, I said as kindly as I could, all different now. He was unhappy too, he was just too proud to admit it.

He said nothing. He got up, walked to the closet, took out his suitcase, packed, and left. He did not even say good-bye, and when I heard him leave I thought for a moment of running to him and asking him to try again, of promising I'd make everything right. But I knew better. I tossed for several hours, trying to sleep. I was still awake at three A.M. when I heard the door open and saw Richard come walking back into the bedroom. He pulled a chair up to the side of the bed, sat down, and looked at me for a few seconds before he spoke.

"I'm not going to give you a divorce," he said finally.

"I can't go on living like this. I can't, Richard. I want a divorce and I'm going through with it." That did it.

In the more than four years I'd been with Richard I'd never seen him lose his temper or be violent in any way. I screamed for help, but none came. When he paused for a moment and began to come to his senses, I made my move, one born of terror, not logic. I told him I'd called Mom after he'd left the first time and that she was driving up from Palm Springs—where she and Pop now lived—to be with me. I said I'd better go telephone her and tell her not to come so that she wouldn't find out what had happened. He nodded.

I pulled on a robe, ran into the living room, telephoned Mom, and told her to call the police. Then I reached down in the crib, scooped up Evan, wrapped her in a blanket, and ran from the apartment. My first instinct was to go to a neighbor's, but it occurred to me that Richard might come looking there first—he knew who I knew in the neighborhood and I didn't want to endanger my neighbors. So I ran down the street and rang an apartment doorbell, the first one I saw with a light on.

The man who answered needed only to look at me. "You want me to call the police?"

"They've been called. But could I use your phone?"

I telephoned Beverly Noga, who had been my manager beginning with *Peyton Place* and who had become a friend as well. I told her what had happened and asked her to come and get me. I also called Mark, who left immediately to help me. Then I waited until I saw the police arrive.

Beverly arrived next, and she walked with me across the street. I held Evan in my arms. Richard was still in a rage. A police officer took me inside and stayed with me while I packed a bag for Evan and myself. Another officer appeared and asked if I wanted to have Richard arrested.

"He's my husband," I wept. "He's the father of my baby."

"That's what makes these things so hard," the officer said. "He is the father of your child and both of you are having a terrible time. I suggest you go with your friend, and hope for the best." I spent the night at Beverly's house and the next day Beverly got me a lawyer.

I was a wreck, a mess inside and out. I went back to the house and discovered Richard had been there ahead of me. A number of things were missing, including his pistol and his sawed-off shotgun. I panicked. Mark came by and made me keep a .38 pistol by my side, but I knew I wouldn't be able to use it. I cannot stand violence of any sort; I can't even swat my pets without feeling remorse.

Mom came up and stayed for a day, but Pop was

having heart trouble again and I urged her to go back to him. I was alone with Evan and so punchy that I was certain I saw Richard drive by several times. I wanted to leave, but I had nowhere to go. Then I remembered something I'd read a few days before in a newspaper, an item about Warren Beatty always keeping a suite at the Beverly Wilshire Hotel, even when he was in New York, as he was now. I picked up the telephone and called Warren at his Manhattan hotel. I asked if I could borrow his suite at the Beverly Wilshire for a few days until things settled down.

Who one likes and dislikes and for what reasons is a subject which fascinates and confuses me. The years Warren had been with Natalie, I had found him thoroughly dislikable. Then, when he had come after me in New York I had found him even more so. I had since seen him several more times, once at a dinner party with Michael, another when my car had broken down and I had run into a nearby restaurant to make a call, and there—with money for the tow truck—was Warren. The legendary Beatty charm had made me a convert, and because he wasn't making Natalie unhappy now I could look upon him in a different light. He was warm, witty, and kind.

"Get over there right now. And stay as long as you'd like," he said. When I arrived at the hotel with Evan and asked for Warren's suite, I was informed that Mr. Beatty was on his way back from New York and that he'd reserved another suite for us. If I'd known he was going to rent another suite, I wouldn't have come. But there I was, and I had nowhere else to go.

Evan and I, with about fifty dollars to our names, moved into the suite in the Beverly Wilshire. I called the house doctor, who came up and put lotion on my bruises. Evan set out to play with every light switch in the place, and I let her do what she wanted. A few hours after we checked in, Mark arrived with my dogs. I didn't want them left alone at the house. The doctor had left some tranquilizers, but I did not take them. Instead, I ordered up a bottle of wine.

The next morning I telephoned Mom and told her where I was. She listened to my story, and when I was done, had only two things to say.

"I'll be right there. And don't tell Natalie."

33

Warren often came to the suite to sit and talk and to offer encouragement. He speaks softly, intensely, and intelligently. People listen. I was constantly struck by the contrast between the Warren I remembered from the days with Natalie and the new Warren. He was thoughtful, considerate, and supportive. I turned to him one day and said I'd pay him back as soon as I had the money, but he waved my offer away with a laugh and said, "After all we've been through, this will make us even. Maybe."

I could not eat. I was finally down to ninety-five pounds before my appetite returned. Evan was an active, curious baby and was—even when she was cranky—a source of solace. So was Mom, who used my trouble as an excuse to leave the desert and come to town for a couple of days whenever she felt it was safe to leave Pop.

I heard nothing from Richard until after I'd gotten an attorney and started divorce proceedings. Then we heard from both Richard and his attorney. Richard's business enterprises were finally doing well, and we'd been living very well for over a year. I assumed reasonable child-support payments and a small alimony check would be forthcoming each month. My lawyer, who had been recommended to me for his savvy in matters just such as this, asked for much more. That's when we all got a big surprise.

Richard was penniless—if the court records were to be believed. I, on the other hand, was an actress accustomed to earning large sums of money and could be counted on to do so as soon as I lifted a telephone to make my availability known. It promised to be a messy divorce and it was. The only thing we didn't disagree on was Evan. He loved her dearly and I wanted her to know her father well; when it came to visitation rights, I wanted him to see her as often as he wanted.

During the divorce, I came back to the hotel one night depressed and confused. Warren appeared with a bottle of wine and a couple of glasses and we sat down to drink. I needed to be loved just a little, to know someone wanted me—and I'm certain I wanted to get back at Richard, too. When Warren leaned across the sofa and kissed me, I offered no resistance. Warren is a passionate and inventive lover, a curator of women whose collection is legendary. For a brief time I became one of them. I worried from time to time that Natalie would find out, but Warren shrugged away my concern and said it wouldn't be from him. It wouldn't be from me either. We kept our secret, shared our wish never to hurt Natalie, even to the extent of never appearing in public together

without others with us. Whatever his motives were,
Warren helped to restore me, gave me shelter and
some of my self-esteem back, and for that I remain
grateful.

My suddenly insolvent ex-husband was finally ordered to pay me $150 a month in child support, and
in the end that is all I got. I didn't even get that
regularly. He lives in Texas now with a new wife and
children, and Evan sees him often. He loves his
daughter, and I ask no more than that.

The actress-in-demand picked up the telephone
and made a painful discovery. She was no longer in
demand, there were plenty of new young girls on the
block, and finding work wasn't going to be easy. I
also began to pay the price for not having actively
pursued my career for the several years I'd taken to
play housewife and then mother, roles I preferred at
the time.

I was also typecast. Finally I landed a good part in a
big television project, *Nightmare in Badham County*, an
ABC Movie of the Week, which gave me a chance to
play what I've come to refer to as the George Ken-
nedy part—real tough.

It was not enough. The bill collector was at my
door, and Evan and I lived on the edge. When I was
absolutely certain money would be coming in within
the next two months—I had a big residual payment
due, big by my standards at the time—I went to Natalie and asked to borrow some money from her to tide
us over. I expected about $3,000 in residuals and so I
asked Natalie to advance me $2,500 and promised to

pay her back. The day I went to her house I was so nervous I was panting. Natalie was cordial and businesslike. We had not been close for a couple of years, and those few times we'd been together had been strained, but I now believed that my predicament might be a way of renewing a relationship with her. It was not, but she did write me a check for $2,500 and I did pay her back within two months.

I dated, but not much. I was now a mother and I was not about to spend the night away, nor was I about to bring anyone home. That was not the example I wanted to set. For months, life was limited to Evan and hoping for more work.

I was introduced to a writer-producer who was in his fifties, and we began dating regularly. No big deal, at least not on my part, just a social encounter with a pleasant man. His name was Alan Balter and within three months he was asking me to marry him. I reported on my record of unsuccessful marriages in some detail and discouraged him.

Finally I married him because I was broke and my prospects for making a good living were dim indeed. I felt I was fortunate that someone loved me, never mind that he wasn't quite who I had in mind as Prince Charming. I had long ago decided I wasn't worthy of who I wanted. I was honest about it, I can say that much to my credit, but I didn't have the guts to go it alone. Too bad. He said love would come eventually, and once again I hoped it would. Even Natalie thought so this time.

Marriage number five lasted less than six months,

and we parted with the understanding we had both made a big mistake. No hard feelings, no recriminations, just a lot of messy paperwork. I asked for nothing, which seemed only fair, given my reasons for marrying him in the first place.

I no sooner left him than I got a short note from Natalie: "And they said it would never last!" she wrote. "I'm sorry, Lana, I really am." Natalie's attempt to smooth over my marital blunder struck me as hilarious, so I called to tell her so.

"But, Lana, why do you keep doing it?" she asked.

"I get married so that I can keep doing it," I cracked.

"You don't have to get married for that. Times have changed."

"That isn't what I was taught. You either."

"Look. You've got to stop believing that stuff. It's taken me years of analysis, but now I don't believe it anymore."

"Here you are, happily married and a mother. And you no longer believe."

She gave a rueful little laugh. "Maybe you only get what you want when you stop believing in it."

I was on my own again, and this time I was determined to make it work. My reconciliation with Natalie had begun. I figured if I could make it on my own, Natalie and I would once again become close. I was right.

34

Natalie and R.J. entertained often and well, usually at dinner parties attended by both the famous and the obscure. The parties could roughly be divided into two categories: Stars and Non-Stars. The Star Parties were more elegant, but not necessarily more fun. All of their friends had interesting lives and had done unusual things; you rarely got stuck in the middle of a dull conversation—and if you did, it was easy enough to move on.

R.J. tended to get involved in conversations and stay with them, while Natalie, determined to be the perfect hostess, moved from group to group. There was a memorable party for Laurence Olivier, with whom Natalie and R.J. made *Cat on a Hot Tin Roof*. Everybody was stiff and formal until Lord Olivier started making cracks and telling everybody to call him Larry. There were about twenty-five or thirty of us there, and only the guest of honor didn't have to remind himself to quit staring in wonder.

That night Natalie stayed up until the last guest left. More often than not, Natalie was in bed before the party was over. As much as she liked to entertain, she also believed in taking care of herself. She was also wise enough to go to bed when she'd had too much to drink—and she often did. She was tiny, so it didn't take much, and she liked her white wine. She also adored a lethal drink called the Scorpion, which was served at Trader Vic's restaurant with a gardenia —also her favorite flower—floating in it. Natalie's capacity lasted somewhere into the second sip of the second drink.

Natalie's routine at parties was carefully established. She'd seldom be downstairs to greet her guests, and would instead come down after most of them had arrived. She was full of small talk, friendly, and a good listener, but when she had had enough— of the party, of the wine, of whatever—she would leave. She would disappear upstairs and then come back down several minutes later, wearing an elegant nightgown and a robe, and explain that she was tired and would be having just one more glass of wine.

"But please, everybody, stay and have a good time."

She'd sit and sip, then off she'd go. Some nights when I was worried she'd had too much to drink I'd wait a few minutes and then go upstairs to see if she was all right. A couple of times I found her in the bathroom throwing up, but usually she was just drifting off to sleep. We'd chat a few seconds, usually talk about the party and who our favorite guests were, and then I'd leave.

R.J., of course, stayed to the last. He is a man who

loves a good party and enjoys playing the host. He, too, likes his drinks, though he can hold them a great deal better than Natalie could.

Early in their remarriage, Natalie was possessive of R.J., wanted to know everything he did, everywhere he went. Mom tells of a day she dropped by when Natalie was in mid-sentence and turned to R.J. for confirmation of a fact. He'd left the room. Natalie immediately demanded to know where he was, called him, and then went looking for him. He was in the little bathroom which served as a guest bathroom, and she stood outside the door and waited for him to come out. She once told me this marriage absolutely had to work, and it was up to her to make it work. Things settled down considerably when she got pregnant, and then after Courtney was born their marriage became much like any other.

She was a housewife with a vengeance, and anything that was necessary to keep R.J. happy was done. When he was working—which was often—she'd fly around the house getting things in order, run into the kitchen to make sure dinner would be ready on time and that his vegetables were cooked as he liked them. I remember any number of occasions seeing Willie Mae, Natalie's long-suffering and beloved housekeeper, look at the ceiling, her patience with the employer she loved so dearly beginning to fray.

Sometimes Natalie and R.J. were homebodies, sometimes they were apart, pursuing their work or their own interests. R. J. was forever giving her gifts, and every time she completed a picture he'd give her another charm for her necklace, a gold disk with the name of the picture and the name of her character engraved on it.

There had been a change in emphasis in their marriage. When they were first married, Natalie had been a major star and R.J. wasn't much more than a handsome man with little experience at acting. Now it was different. Natalie was still a movie star, of course, and in the Hollywood caste system that made her a much bigger star than any television star, which is what R.J. was. She had her scripts, all bound in leather, on display in her bookcase. She had a past, and it was a glorious one. He had the present, and it was more glamorous than glorious. It wasn't lost on anyone in show business that R.J. wasn't *just* a television star; he was in his third hit series and he was making a fortune. Natalie was a film star who wasn't working much.

When she did work, R.J. would go out of his way to pay attention to her. She was shooting *The Last Married Couple in America* and had invited me to lunch on my birthday. R.J. came too and the three of us ate in the studio commissary. R.J. was attentive to the point of saying, "Yes, darling," every time she spoke. Natalie didn't seem to react at all, except to take it as her due. I was a bit uncomfortable with it. After lunch we all walked back to her trailer, with R.J. dutifully carrying the leftover birthday cake. I said good-bye, kissed them both on the cheek, and took the cake from R.J.

"Where are you parked, Lana?"

"About three stages away," I said, pointing down

the long alley between the soundstages. Three stages isn't far away at all.

"R.J., go get Lana's car for her. It's her birthday, after all," Natalie said.

I pointed out I could walk the short distance without any trouble, even volunteered it was worth my while, considering the cake I'd just consumed.

"Absolutely not," Natalie ordered. "R.J., get the car. Lana, give him your keys."

"You're the movie star, darling. Anything you want," R.J. said. He meant it, too. R.J. went and got my car and when I climbed in, I thanked him and then added a special thanks for his being so considerate to Natalie.

"It was nothing," he said, then quickly turned and walked away.

There were other changes in Natalie, changes which seemed to be both concessions to changing times and Natalie's desire to be *au courant.* An actress turned producer, who had been a close friend of Natalie's, once sat down in Natalie's living room and smoked a joint. Natalie was furious and terminated the friendship. Now, years later, Natalie stood by at a party at her house as a well-known actor inhaled his second joint. This time Natalie's two daughters were watching. Natalie said nothing.

The girls asked me what he was doing, and I explained as best I could. Later I asked Natalie how she felt about it.

"It's no big deal. I've tried it a couple of times and

I don't like it, but that's pretty much it. You ever done it?"

"Very little. I don't like it either."

Her disapproval of swearing also vanished and Natalie herself became a colorful cusser. The first time I heard her spew a string of expletives I was so astonished I started giggling. We had both been taught never to swear. Years of being in show business, where nearly everybody swears, hadn't changed us a bit. Now Natalie had succumbed. Certain women can swear and get away with it. Englishwomen can utter the most profane words and make them sound totally acceptable. Natalie couldn't quite pull it off with the panache of the British, but she managed fairly well. I was frankly impressed and told her so. Within weeks of discovering Natalie's new use of the language I was beginning to cuss a bit myself. It was an odd use of a maxim I had learned as a child: if it was something Natalie did, it was okay for me to do it too.

35

In the past, on those rare occasions when I would decide to go directly to Natalie to ask why she was angry with me—my hand sweating as I held the telephone—the dialogue would go something like this:

"Natalie, Mom says you're mad at me. You haven't returned my calls for a couple of weeks and I haven't seen you so I wondered what was going on." I'd get it all out in one very long sentence, certain that if I paused I'd fall apart.

"I don't have any problem. If you think there's a problem, then perhaps it's your problem."

This wasn't only psychoanalytic claptrap. We had been taught all of our lives not to talk about problems. Natalie had held hers back for years, but now they began to come out.

It started on those afternoons when Natalie would ring and ask Evan and me to come over. Evan and Courtney, usually accompanied by Natasha, would go out into the yard to play, and Natalie and I would retire to her bar, the room in the big house on Canon Drive she was most comfortable in. The house was

New England in style, and Natalie, with her love of colors and R.J.'s sure taste, decorated it beautifully. They had come a long way from that gold-and-white turkey. The living room was adorned by her beloved Bonnard, but the bar, with its traditional family pictures and framed prints of ships, was where she loved to sit and talk. It was a cozy little room, actually not much more than a hallway leading from the living room to the den. The bar stools, heavy wood with leather backing, had been bought during her first marriage to R.J. When they divorced, R.J. gave them to his sister. When they remarried, his sister returned them. It was a story Natalie liked to repeat to friends.

Perched on the stools, we'd ramble on, mostly about raising our daughters, but also about acting. Once she astonished me by saying she was about to go on the Merv Griffin show and was utterly terrified. She was used to speaking words from a script, she said. She was not at all spontaneous on such occasions, and had been very nervous about the Griffin show—was even considering canceling—when she figured out just exactly what to do.

"What?" I asked, curious to know her secret.

"I'm going to pretend I'm you!"

"I don't understand."

"Lana, I've never known anyone else who had an answer for every question asked under pressure."

"Me?"

"I have always been envious of that. I mean, you've always got something to say. Usually funny."

I thought that was terrific and said so. Natalie just laughed.

"I always thought you were the one who knew what to say."

"Fooled ya," she laughed again.

As our lives changed, our responsibilities increased, a sort of trust built between us, a trust founded in part on understanding and in part on Natalie's sympathy for my troubles as a single mother raising a child with little in the way of financial help from Evan's father. Natalie never offered me money, never so much as brought the subject up, but she was always curious to know how things were going and her attention seldom faltered as I answered her questions.

I lived in a small apartment not far from her house, and one morning, a little after one A.M., there was a terrific commotion outside my door. I could hear two people giggling, and then my doorbell rang. It was Natalie and R.J., thoroughly in their cups and having the time of their lives. They were, Natalie explained, in the neighborhood and decided to drop by to say hello. I was at first a bit irritated at being gotten up in the middle of the night just to say hello, but their infectious good mood soon caught me too and before long we were sitting around giggling. It was the first time either of them had ever come to where I lived, and I noticed that, even slightly drunk, Natalie missed nothing. I had two dogs and one of them, a mixture of West Highland white, poodle, and who knows what else, immediately took to R.J. He was a scruffy little blond pup, very friendly, and I'd named him Potatoes. R.J. took to Potatoes and threatened to make off with him. After about an hour Natalie began to fade and they got up to leave. As they started out the door, I scooped up Potatoes and handed him to R.J.

"He's obviously meant for you," I said to R.J.

R.J. took the wiggling little creature into his arms, kissed me on the cheek, and Potatoes went to live in a big house in Beverly Hills, where he became one of a menagerie of five dogs, several cats, and a slew of chickens which were kept in a pen at the side of the house. Natalie, who was compulsively neat about everything, had long ago given up on keeping her back lawn free of messes. She referred to them as land mines and told anyone who ventured out there that they did so at their own risk. Nor was she an especially good disciplinarian with her animals. She would make a stab at training each new dog, but then R.J. would take over. If R.J. didn't make a go of it, they called in outside help. Still, Natalie once reminded me, she was a stern taskmaster compared to Marilyn Monroe. Natalie, it seemed, had once gone to visit Marilyn to see Marilyn's beloved new pet, a big boxer. The dog went to the bathroom wherever he wished and also chewed on the furniture. Each time the dog misbehaved, Marilyn would reach for her box of Kleenex, pull out a tissue, and slap the dog on the face with it. Natalie's imitation of Marilyn slapping her big dog with a Kleenex was one of her best.

Natalie worked, but not as often as she'd have liked. At a time when she was actively looking for a picture, she was offered the role of Daisy in *The Great Gatsby*, playing opposite her good friend Robert Redford. There was one condition, however, and it proved insurmountable. If she wanted the part she would have to do a screen test. To ask this of an established star, one with miles—a whole lifetime, in this case—of film to her credit, was too much for Natalie's pride. She refused. Several years later she was offered a role in an Agatha Christie murder, *The Mirror Crack'd*, playing an aging and impossibly vain movie star. Natalie read the script, put it down, and started swearing. She would not, she said, stoop to such shit. She was not yet old enough to be looked upon as aging, and she refused, absolutely refused to play such parts. Elizabeth Taylor did it.

What was painfully clear was that those few offers that were forthcoming were not really very good at all. We all knew what was happening, and Natalie—who tended to keep her troubles to herself—made no attempt to hide her dismay or, in the case of *Gatsby* and *The Mirror Crack'd*, her rage. One night we were sitting around her bar, sipping wine and talking about our careers, a somewhat unusual topic because when we were together we tended to talk about our children.

"I want to produce a movie for television. That's what I want to do," I said at one point. Natalie nodded, then was silent for a moment. She ran an elegant finger with a small diamond ring on it down the side of the glass, making a small trail in the condensation.

"You know what I want? I want yesterday," she said finally.

She made an attempt to join that legion of busy Beverly Hills housewives who divide their time between shopping, fashionable lunches, beauty parlors, and charitable causes. She approached this phase of her life with typical vigor and chose as her companion Wendy Goldberg, the wife of producer Leonard Goldberg and a woman known for being on the boards of every acceptable cause.

"Wendy is a doer," Natalie said. "She'll find the right charity and I'll become a charity mogul."

Then began a round of lunches, meetings, and dinners with Wendy and Wendy's friends. R.J. participated with enthusiasm, in part because Leonard Goldberg was one of the producers of *Hart to Hart.*

Natalie and I went out to lunch one day after this great burst of activity and I asked her how it was all going.

"You know what Wendy Goldberg is?" Natalie asked. I thought it was a rhetorical question and kept quiet. I thought "She's a doer" was the answer.

"She's a bore," Natalie said. "She doesn't mean to be, but when you're a rich housewife involved in charitable causes, your range is pretty narrow. I'm not fit for this sort of thing." The Wendy Goldberg lunches ceased shortly thereafter, but the two did remain casual friends because of their husbands' business association.

Natalie felt her children came first, at least for the first years of their lives; the majority of her time was spent being a mother. She was a mother who did not cook, which was occasionally the source of family jokes. Natalie, someone once said, was a real space cadet when it came time to go into a kitchen. She was the first to agree. On Willie Mae's days off, Chez Wagner ate either to-go or snacked on what Willie Mae, in her infinite wisdom, left behind for her starving charges. R.J. and the girls all liked a big breakfast, but not Natalie. In time, R.J. became something of an expert at whipping together Sunday breakfasts.

Natalie had a nanny, a maid, and all of the other trappings of success, but she supervised her children closely and always made a point of including Katie Wagner, R.J.'s daughter, as one of the family. It wasn't hard to do. Katie was a sweet, friendly child who has grown into a lovely young woman. Natasha Gregson is a lively child who has the good looks of both her parents, and all of Natalie's enthusiasm. Courtney is very blond, and looks surprisingly like her stepsister. Courtney is also an extremely spirited child, a tomboy who loves a dare and looks constantly for adventure. I once told Natalie that of all the things she'd done in her life, she raised children the best.

R.J. too. He is a doting, attentive father. Natalie sometimes got impatient with her daughters and even on occasion yelled a bit. Not R.J. His patience with his daughters was infinite. While Natalie welcomed Katie as a member of the family, R.J. did the same with Natasha. They were a close clan. For a while, until Natalie was gone, Evan was often included in the Wagner family adventures, something Natalie realized was important to Evan's sense of her family—Natalie's daughters are the only cousins she knows—and she still sees them occasionally, usually when her grandmother takes her around. I almost never see them, a situation which is not my choice but is certainly my circumstance.

36

One of the reasons Natalie and I grew closer near the end of her life is Alan Feinstein, the man with whom I have been involved over four years now. Alan is an actor, and a serious one. He won the Drama Desk Award for best supporting actor in *A View from the Bridge* during the 1983 Broadway season. Alan is definitely not Hollywood, something that endeared him to Natalie when they met. *View from the Bridge* was directed by Arvin Brown, who was introduced to Alan by Natalie. It was Arvin who was to direct Natalie's stage debut in *Anastasia*.

Alan was in the kitchen helping me cook dinner one night when he turned around and asked if I'd ever invited Natalie to my place for dinner.

I think I was as surprised by his question as he was by my answer. No, I had not. I virtually never saw Natalie where I lived. I saw her at her house, and at her invitation. I didn't wait to be summoned and I knew I was now welcome, but it had honestly never occurred to me to invite Natalie and R.J. to dinner. For one thing, I was terrified she'd say no. So, never one to flinch in the face of a challenge, Alan insisted he'd cook a big gourmet dinner at his apartment in Hollywood, but only if I invited Natalie and R.J.

Alan cooked an elaborate and elegant duck dinner and Natalie arrived first, followed a bit later by R.J., who was working. It was the sort of night which made me wonder why I'd waited so long. We laughed, talked, drank wine, and there was about the whole evening a sense of ease, of trust. When they left, I helped Alan wash the dishes, and I kept shaking my head in awe.

There were the occasional bumps, but by and large those last several years went well for us all.

We were all at their house, watching the kids swim, when R.J. and Alan decided to swim too. So did Natalie. Not wanting to be left out, I got on my swimsuit too. I walked out of the guesthouse and toward the pool as R.J. glanced up and looked me over.

"I suppose I'll be walking around with a hard-on for the rest of the afternoon," he said. Natalie's flash of anger, first at him, and then her quick look at me, was not lost on anyone. She said nothing until I was in the pool, sitting on the bottom step, and then she came and sat down beside me.

"Did you have your tits done?"

"Done?" I wasn't sure if she was implying a lift or enlargement.

"Done," she said emphatically, refusing to believe I didn't quite understand.

"Same old tits," I replied. I wanted to go home and hide.

On another occasion the kids were jumping in and out of the pool and Natalie ran into the house and came back out with a camera. She took pictures of the kids and then one of R.J. and me. When she handed R.J. the camera so that he could take a picture of the two of us, he looked into the view-finder then looked directly at me.

"I've got to get this just right so Lana can send them to Richard so they can sell them and make money."

"R.J., that's in the past now. It's all forgotten," Natalie countered.

"Not by me it isn't," R.J. shot back. Natalie patted me on the arm and shook her head.

Mom, who had always been a strong presence in our lives, now reemerged as a force we both had to reckon with. Pop's health continued to fail and on November 5, 1980, his heart finally gave out. Mom, true to form, went into hysterics and it required the services of a doctor, a nurse, and all three of her daughters to get her going again. Natalie wrote the eulogy with some help from me. She had resolved her feelings about Pop. I had not. While Natalie kept a firm grip on herself during the days he was dying, I slipped from time to time. Working with her on the eulogy, she said, would help me with my grief. I had to go to therapy over Natalie's eulogy. Pop wasn't dead yet and here was Natalie already planning his funeral. Film friends were to be present. She looked on this as a performance, and every performance to her was critical. Natalie decided to use a quotation from her moving classroom speech in *Splendor in the Grass* the Wordsworth lines:

> *What though the radiance which was once so bright*
> *Be now forever taken from my sight,*
> *Though nothing can bring back the hour*
> *Of splendour in the grass, of glory in the flower;*
> *We will grieve not, rather find*
> *Strength in what remains behind.*

I felt uneasy about the selection. When Pop finally did die, and I was in the chapel listening to Natalie's eulogy, I realized she was indulging her private feelings rather than attempting to express what Pop was all about. He was a conservative, traditional White Russian who loved to read history and fact, not poetry and novels. I used to fight with him about fiction being an extension of the self, but he never saw that fantasy was valid. Right or wrong, he was entitled to be accurately represented at his funeral.

Natalie felt he should have a wooden coffin because he had been an unpretentious workingman and a carpenter. I couldn't live with that. Why not give Pop something better?

Our biggest problem was dealing with Mom. Natalie owned a condominium in West Los Angeles and had arranged for Mom and Pop to live there as long as they'd like. Now Mom was certain she'd have to move and it took some time to convince her otherwise. We took turns taking her in, sometimes for weeks at a time, and it wasn't long before Mom came to expect to be with one or the other of us at all times.

Nor was it long before Mom was back at her elaborate intrigues, but this time she made the mistake of playing politics Chez Wagner, and less than six months after Pop was gone, Natalie had had enough.

The first I heard of it was when Mom called, sobbing, saying that Natalie had thrown her out of the house, bag and baggage. She was at the bus stop at the corner of Canon Drive and Santa Monica Boulevard, two blocks from Natalie's house. I quickly got on the phone to Natalie, who, through tears and a clenched jaw, said that Mom's playing off one child against the other, all of them against R.J. and her, simply had to stop. She'd warned Mom, but to no avail.

I jumped in my car and found Mom, my tiny Mom, standing with two suitcases, blowing her nose. She wailed that Natalie was mistreating her, and I listened, knowing full well Natalie was forgiven no matter what she did. I took her home with me and put her to bed. Within two days Mom and Evan were fighting and I knew it wouldn't last long at my apartment either.

"Promise me," Natalie said on the phone a few days later. "Promise me that whatever happens you'll never let Mom live with you. She's taken care of. If she lives with you, there will only be trouble."

It was a promise I fully intended to keep. I kept it, too, until Natalie was gone, and then I couldn't find it in my heart to give Mom the boot. By then we were all she had. She still lives with me from time to time, and still has her condominium. She is alternately loving and disruptive, which is to say she is really no different than she ever was.

Natalie later swore Mom's games had caused a row between her and R.J., and I think she spoke the truth. In all the years of their second marriage, I never once heard an angry exchange between Natalie and R.J. They had arguments—they both admitted that—and Natalie once told me that some of them were whoppers, but never in front of their children, their family, or their friends. R.J. once remarked that Natalie waited until later to get even whenever she got angry at him. What was clear was that they had settled into a long marriage, one that for all appearances was a happy one. She said to me once that with R.J., especially the second time around, she knew what she was getting into. When I asked her to elaborate, she shrugged her shoulders and changed the subject by saying, "This time it'll work. It's got to."

I think they would have stayed married even if the marriage had turned into a disaster. They had to live out the dream the world had imagined for them, whether or not it went sour.

Their tradition of big Thanksgiving dinners and formal New Year's Eve dinners continued. In 1977 Natalie made a film called *Meteor*, which wasn't successful with either the critics or the audiences, but which did initiate a friendship between Natalie and Sean Connery. Sean had remarried since I had seen him last, and since he had spent the last week I worked with him refusing to speak to me, I arrived for Thanksgiving that year wondering how he'd react. I had told Natalie and had even offered not to come, but she persisted. I arrived with Evan, who was a very shy child, especially around men. Sean greeted me like a long-lost friend, but it was to Evan that he directed his charm, and to my delight Evan responded. Within fifteen minutes Evan, who circled strangers warily, was in his lap and whispering in his ear.

"You've changed," Sean said to me later that evening.

"So have you."

Diamonds Are Forever and Plenty O'Toole seemed only dim memories of another time and another life. I found Sean a delight, and went away wishing we'd first met under better circumstances.

The Wagners' Thanksgiving dinners were informal family affairs. Their New Year's Eve bashes were strictly black-tie. They were grand celebrations and I looked forward to them every year. Natalie forbade any mention of year-end depressions, of unrealized dreams, of anything which would detract from her intent for the evening: be happy, have a wonderful time. We usually did. One year Mart Crowley had a bit too much to drink—a good bit too much—and Natalie took him aside and ordered him to stop. She looked at me—one of her come-and-help looks—and I went and sat with Mart. Later, when he decided to leave, I accompanied him to the door.

"You can take one step, just one, to either side of the line Natalie draws for you," he said, "but if you take two steps you're in big trouble. You ought to know, Lana, you've been over the line a few times yourself."

"I know. I've been there a lot. I just can never understand why."

"Natalie likes to be in control," he said, putting on his coat. "Or else."

I continued to work erratically, mostly in television. I also made a picture which was first shown with the title *Dark Eyes*. It was so bad the producers released it under several different titles around the nation. People came up to me and said, "I saw you in such-and-so," and that's how I would discover the latest title of *Dark Eyes*, a horror film in every sense.

Nonetheless I'm grateful to *Dark Eyes* for two things. It inadvertently provided me with the best night out I'd ever spent with Natalie—and it spurred me to think about changing careers.

It's impossible to tell just how a film is going while it is being made. All of us involved with *Dark Eyes* felt we had a shot at making an unusual horror picture, one that might one day evolve into a cult film of sorts. The script seemed good, the elements were all there. They just never came together, something none of us discovered until the night it was given a starry preview and I invited Natalie and R.J. to come with me. Natalie turned it into an event and insisted we all go directly from the screening and cocktail party to dinner at the Bistro Garden, one of the "in" gathering spots in Beverly Hills, which both Natalie and I happened to like. It is an elegant place, with flowered wallpaper, dark wood paneling, candlelight, and European-style service. The feeling is one of being special, and this was to be a special night. Alan, meanwhile, decided a limousine would be in order. The only crimp in the plan was R.J., who had to miss the screening because of a late shooting schedule on *Hart to Hart.* He promised he'd meet us at the restaurant.

There was champagne before the screening and my nerves must have shown because as the lights dimmed to signal us all into the theater, the bartender walked over and handed me a full bottle and three glasses. Natalie, Alan, and I sipped our way through this bomb while I fought to keep from getting sick, and resisted the urge to leave. Once or twice Natalie reached over and patted me on the arm, but it was clear within the first fifteen minutes that we'd created a monster.

When it was over, we raced for the limousine. Natalie offered all the encouragement she could find, and she had managed to remember every reasonable move I'd made and commented on them all. I just waved it all away and suggested we go on to dinner as though nothing had happened.

We ordered wine and then dinner. Neither Natalie nor I got what we thought we ordered, and so the waiter, eager to please, brought us the menus so that we could choose something else. Natalie looked up over her menu and grinned wickedly. She was engaging me in a conspiracy because my film had disappointed me so, and I happily went along. We ordered a lot and, wonder of wonders, since neither of us has large appetites, we ate it all.

R.J. and Alan began talking about their careers, a long discussion having to do with the differences between being a celebrity and an actor. R.J., Alan insisted, could create a presence just by stepping on a set. Alan, R.J. contended, could do things R.J. would never dream of trying. And on and on they went. Given the fact that Natalie and I also shared professions with them, it would have been perfectly natural for us to join in the conversation.

We didn't. Instead, we began talking about our childhood, our shared memories. Natalie wore a jacket and a skirt of green and gold cut velvet, tight-fitting and slit up the sides. She looked stunning. I wore a plain black dress with long sleeves with an open back that was draped to the waist. I looked stunning too. We began with our clothes and worked back from there.

And we sipped wine as we went. Natalie paused once and listened to the piano player, then turned to me and said, "Do you remember when we used to sing along with the Barbra Streisand records?" I did. We used to do what aspiring singers all over the world did: try to sound like Streisand. Because my sister was Natalie Wood, movie star, we had better equipment. We had a tape recorder and earphones to attach to the record player, so we not only got to sing like Streisand, we got to hear what we sounded like. We sounded terrible. At the time it was a terrible blow to our musical egos, but that night at the Bistro Garden it was a rollicking memory.

We talked about Mom and about Pop, and we mourned the fact that Pop hadn't lived a longer, happier life. We talked about our daughters, and they, once again, led us back to our childhood. Natalie brought up my fall from the horse and her horrible guilt feelings over it, and I comforted her. I reeled off my litany of bad behavior and apologized for everything, and she reached over and put her arm around me.

We talked about relationships, especially with the men in our lives, and this was something Natalie understood very well.

"They love us because we're feminine and dependent and pretty," she whispered. "They haven't any idea just how strong we are. I know R.J. hasn't."

We talked about our own relationship, our ups, our downs, the long period of estrangement. No excuses were offered, no apologies were made, it was just all right out there for the first time. I was stammering my way through a recitation about how much I had missed her during the difficult time—I remember using exactly those two words.

"You know, I always wanted to be exactly like you," I said. "It took such a long time before I could understand and accept that it wasn't possible. God, it gave us all such trouble."

"But it *was* impossible," Natalie said. "It was wrong that you were expected to do what I did. What happened to me was a fluke. It couldn't happen twice. Not in the same family."

"It wasn't just that it was expected. I wanted it, too. It has taken all of my life—until just recently—for me to begin to connect with who I really am, to accept my own values and my own life as worthwhile. I'm so glad it finally happened." I was on the verge of tears.

With that, she pulled me to her and said, "I love you."

"I love you, too." We both began weeping.

Neither Alan nor R.J. had paid any attention to us until they saw us in one another's arms crying. Then they asked what the matter was.

"Nothing, nothing at all," Natalie stammered. "We're making up for lost time."

"We're happy. These are happy tears," I told them.

And they were. I don't know what I would do if I didn't have the memory of this evening to comfort me. It took place during a cold wintry California night early in 1981. Natalie was gone before the year ended.

37

It was a time of change for both of us. Natalie was preparing to move out of the world of mothering and back into the world of acting. The children were in school, and working to Natalie was second nature. She knew it wasn't going to be easy and was certain more insults like *Gatsby* and *The Mirror Crack'd* lay ahead, but she said she was reconciled to things like that. *The Last Married Couple in America* had bombed at the box office, as had the two films she made before it. Natalie, as she so aptly put it, was "right up against it."

Her work in television had been more successful. She followed 1979's *Cat on a Hot Tin Roof* with *From Here to Eternity,* recreating the part played in the film by Deborah Kerr. This time she fared well both critically and in the ratings.

Still, it was not an easy time for her. She wanted to work, but the work wasn't always there when she wanted it. She plunged into the world of television by reading surveys, ratings, and anything else that would teach her how the industry worked. R.J., who has a natural bent toward business, television in particular, also helped her.

So did I, though one afternoon I had to confess to her that I felt a bit silly coaching a major star about the perils of working in television. She, in turn, helped me make a major decision about my life. *Dark Eyes* had convinced me of one thing: I had better look for work elsewhere than in acting. I felt my future was limited, I was typecast, and I had a child in private school to support. Evan had been tested early on in her school years and was found to be gifted, which meant she should have special education. The carefree days were over. I still looked good with a tan, but there wasn't time to get one, not anymore.

Natalie and I made a list of the things I was good at. I had no secretarial skills, nor was I particularly mathematical, so that eliminated work as a script supervisor or a director's assistant. What it came down to was that I was extremely well read. I was not overly educated, I had no special training other than as an actress. It seems odd to contemplate now, but the obvious did not occur to either of us for some time. I was naturally suited to production, finding stories and getting them on course toward becoming films or movies-of-the-week. It was a business only slightly less volatile than acting, and there were even fewer jobs.

"I could go to work as an assistant on *Hart to Hart*," I volunteered hopefully. Natalie didn't answer. She put her finger to her chin in deep thought and then announced: "With all the people you know, finding a job shouldn't be too hard."

It was an awkward moment, but one that I had precipitated. I had never in my life asked Natalie to get me a job, not even to arrange an introduction to someone who might get me one. Mom used to tell me that Natalie would say no one would ever be able to claim Lana got a job because of her sister, that whatever I got it'd be on my own. It became a source of pride. But now it was time for a change, and I knew —she had done it for others and so had R.J.—that it required only a phone call or two and I would be on my way to collecting my first credit in a new profession. *Hart to Hart,* for instance, was frequently behind in the production of scripts and could have used help. Salary was no great problem, I'd work for little just to get my foot in the door. The credit sheet for the show is chockablock with their friends. It would not, however, contain the name of any blood relative.

Natalie was right about one thing, though. I did know a lot of people. I got on the phone and started making appointments. I bought some businesslike clothes, started reading *Publishers Weekly,* and hoped for the best. It took several weeks, but my constant thumbing through my phone book and my pestering paid off. I was hired by Ron Samuels, the producer and—at the time—husband of Lynda Carter. They needed a production assistant who was only slightly more important than a secretary. I had a desk in a corner of a busy office and I plunged in with a vigor which I'm certain drove Ron to distraction from time to time. I was supposed to keep track of several projects in development, and occasionally come up with ideas. Ideas, even in television, do not occur minute by minute, but on some days they whipped out of my typewriter at that rate.

I even got some on-the-line production experience on several Lynda Carter specials. No great shakes from an artistic standpoint, but a good lesson in the business that is television. Then, one day, just like in one of those old Busby Berkeley movies—go out there an unknown and come back a star—I got my break. Ron's development person left and the job was open. I got it. My salary barely changed, but the level of responsibility certainly did. From that, and from observing the other people I met who did what I did, I learned one of the basic rules of television: keep moving. The turnover is fast, the pace of the job even faster. Middle-level executives in television rise and fall by the adroitness of their ability to move from job to job. Ron was no different from any other producer in television. He was volatile, unsure how the networks would treat him from day to day, and given to fits of great frustration. It went with the territory, which is why there are some rather peculiar people in the business. The mix of business with creativity is at the best of times an uneasy one. In television it is never the best of times. I was learning.

One day Ron said something which caused my heart to sink. The subject of who was bankable and who was not bankable in television came up. Ron listed several television stars who were powerful enough to get a project going. I expressed surprise that the list was so short.

"Not even Natalie," he said.

I said nothing. Natalie was a star, she always had been, and she would be forever. It was a fact of my childhood, one that had accompanied me into adult life.

"She's not enough to get a picture going without a big name to go with her," he continued. "Like I said, it's a changing business."

I refused to believe him. I went back to my office and sat there staring at my desk. It couldn't be. Then a terrible thought came to me. Did Natalie know? Natalie, who knew the business backward and forward? Of course she did. She knew it all, and all of a sudden I understood the changes of mood, the edge she had from time to time. She was beautiful, she was talented, she was famous. She was an actress, and time was taking its inevitable toll.

Sitting there at my desk, I suddenly understood a lot of things, things which had shaded our relationship over the years. I understood why she acted as she sometimes did, why the pressure of a needy little sister might at times be too much, why there was refuge in marriage and motherhood, why it was she seemed to be trying to transform herself into something of a social arbiter in the business. I twiddled a pencil, and several times I reached for the telephone to call her, just to say hello and that I was thinking of her.

She wasn't there. She was off doing something

connected with Natasha's school, then she was going to lunch, then an appointment. Natalie kept busy, no doubt about it.

I underestimated Natalie. While I worried, Natalie made her moves. She found a film, signed for it, and got ready to go back to work. It was called *Brainstorm.* Her leading man would be Christopher Walken, one of the hot young actors in town. That wasn't all. Natalie decided she would take a big risk. She agreed to make her first appearance in the theater, to star in a production of *Anastasia.* It would open in Los Angeles and if everything worked out, the play would move on to New York and Broadway. It was the beginning of a new phase in her life. Natalie was nervous—"scared shitless" was how she explained what she felt. She was also full of optimism.

She decided to take the est training and went to Esalen with her *Brainstorm* dress designer Donfeld. Natalie made new friends, stayed in their cottage, and invited me to come up. She was the kind of person who never stopped growing, who had no intention of dying then or ever.

38

Thanksgiving 1981, we all assembled at Natalie's and R.J.'s, a mix of family and friends grown together over years of dinners. This one was not really like the others. There was something off about it, some intangible difference which, given all that was to happen during the days after it, I didn't think about a great deal except to wonder what was going on as Evan, Mom, and I drove home. Mom too remarked on it.

Natalie was wearing a purple angora sweater with silver threads running through it and matching purple slacks and shoes. She looked lovely. She was also incredibly tense, a very different Natalie from the one I had last seen just before she was to start shooting *Brainstorm*. It was a film she looked upon as a way of maybe rescuing a faltering film career and one that would get her stage career off to a good start. She was thrilled to be working, and nervous, too.

"That's okay," I told her when she complained of her anxiety. "That means you really care what you're doing."

"That's one way of looking at it." She smiled.

Natalie was a bundle of nerves. Mart was there, so was R.J.'s mother, Chat Wagner. Delphine Mann and Peggy Griffin, family friends of Natalie's, were there. Delphine is the former wife of Delbert Mann, a director, and Peggy first came into Natalie's life as her secretary and then went on to work for a producing-directing team and remained Natalie's friend. About twelve in all, though many people came and went during the course of the afternoon and evening.

Natalie's first concern after we were all present was that the fireplace wasn't working right, the fire wasn't big enough. Then she'd sit for a few minutes, only to fly into action—lighting her fragrant Rigaud candles, only to race about putting them out a few minutes later. She had little scented cardboard circles that she placed on the lights of various lamps. The heat from the lightbulb released the scent. At least four times that I can recall, Natalie scurried around the room making sure they were working.

R.J. was his usual affable self, moving around fixing drinks and acting as though everything was going according to schedule. Chris Walken came by, spoke briefly to R.J. and to Natalie, but didn't have much to say to anybody else. He left in less than two hours.

Finally the buffet dinner was served, and afterward, as we all sat around, the last of the food still on our plates, Natasha came running up behind Natalie, who was sitting on her big brocade sofa in front of the fireplace.

"Mommy, please don't go this weekend. I feel bad I can't come with you. Go another time."

"Natasha, you've made plans with your friends that you can't cancel, and R.J. and I have our plans too. You're going to go through with your plans and we're going through with ours."

That was it, a brief exchange between a mother and a daughter which normally would have meant nothing, a quick conversation I would have completely forgotten except for what was to come.

"R.J. and I are going out on the boat for a couple of days," she explained. "Chris Walken is coming with us. The weather should be perfect."

Then, one by one, she asked her friends to join them for the weekend. Mart said he had to work on *Hart to Hart* but would like a rain check. Peggy Griffin and her boyfriend pleaded the press of work, and so did Delphine Mann. Natalie did not issue me an invitation, though she certainly knew I loved boats, fishing, and diving. It was a part of her life in which my side of her family was never included, and it was something I had come to accept without ever knowing the reasons for it. It was just there, and I honestly don't even remember feeling awkward that several others were asked in my presence and I was not.

Natalie asked after Alan, who was back east in a play, and I responded by asking her how the film was going.

"You know how aging actresses make horror films? You know, *Whatever Happened to Baby Jane?* and that kind of thing?"

I nodded.

"Well, this is my way of doing something like that. Only this one isn't a horror film. It's a contemporary horror film," she said, carefully putting the emphasis on "contemporary." "It's science fiction. Me and all those magnificent special effects."

"Oh, c'mon, Natalie. This is a long, long way from *Whatever Happened to Baby Jane.* Those were two women—probably in their early sixties when they made it—playing two old hags. Hardly the same thing."

"I just wonder how different it really is."

"A lot. A very big lot."

Later that night Mom and I discussed the party and tried to pin down what was wrong, what was off about the evening. Neither of us could figure it out.

"Something's going on with Natalie," Mom guessed. "I wonder what."

39

The call came at eight o'clock Sunday morning on the long Thanksgiving weekend. I had spent a restless night and at one point Mom, who wasn't sleeping well either, and I got up and went to the kitchen for a snack. I had what Natalie and I used to call "shpilkes," a vaguely Russian-Jewish word for being antsy. The call was from Sheri Herman, a girl I had met in second grade and who had been a good friend ever since. I heard the ring and pulled my head farther under the covers. Mom jumped out of her bed and answered it.

"Lana, it's Sheri. You want to talk to Sheri?"

"Tell her I'll call her later," I said, and promptly went back to sleep.

Ten minutes later Sheri called again. This time I answered it.

"Sheri, I've been up all night and I'm exhausted. I'll call you later." I didn't even wait for her to protest.

The next time the phone rang, Evan answered it. I

heard her say, "Mommy's still in bed. I'll tell her when she wakes up."

The next time Sheri called, Mom answered. I was now waking up, vaguely aware that something was wrong. I heard Mom say, "Sheri, what is wrong? You sound terrible." Then there was a long pause, a pause which ended when Mom began screaming, stopping only long enough to say, "Are you sure? Are you sure?"

I jumped out of bed and grabbed my phone, and from where I was standing I watched as Mom sagged and collapsed on the floor.

Sheri said she had heard a report on the radio which said that Natalie's body had washed up on shore on Catalina Island.

I knew Natalie had gone to Catalina after Thanksgiving, but I told my friend Sheri, "That's impossible. There's obviously been a big mistake. Let's wait and see what happens."

I thanked Sheri and hung up. I was cool, calm, and collected, but not for long. I got Mom onto the living-room couch, made her some tea, and talked her into staying conscious, insisting all the time that there had been some gigantic mix-up and that unless there was some official call of some sort we had nothing to worry about.

Then my old friend Bob Bell called. "Go downstairs and get some coffee going," he said. "I'll be right over."

"Is it true?"

"I think so."

"Oh, God." For the first time my voice broke. Mom, who had gotten off the sofa and come to stand near me, collapsed on the floor again. This time when I tried to revive her she wouldn't come to. Bob arrived as I was calling the paramedics. Evan reacted immediately by running upstairs and locking herself in the bathroom. I began sobbing uncontrollably.

My memories of the next several hours are hazy. Several more people arrived. I do remember trying to get Evan out of the bathroom, but not succeeding until Suzanne Miller, a wonderful young girl who had worked briefly as Evan's nanny while I was making *Dark Eyes*, arrived and took charge. Mom came to briefly and began screaming, then completely lost consciousness.

I remember the paramedics telling us that Mom's blood pressure was over two hundred and that she needed a doctor's services. So, with everything else going on around me, I started looking for a doctor for Mom. She had chronic high blood pressure, she even had medicine for it, but where she got it, I never knew, because she did not have a doctor. I became obsessed with finding her a doctor, I think in part because it gave me some definite direction to move in and in part out of a terror of having to face another death.

My sister Olga called and said she and her husband and two of their sons would fly down in a couple of hours. I invited them all to stay with me. I wanted as many people around me as possible and I thought that might help Mom as well. I was certain it would help Evan. She adored her Aunt Olga, who by this time had grandchildren younger than Evan.

There was no doubting it now. By the time Olga and Alexi arrived we knew it was certain; we'd watched the helicopter bearing her body leave Catalina and come to the mainland. We'd heard reports on the radio and on television. Finally, R.J. called. He had stayed behind in Catalina and then flown home with her body.

"What happened, R.J.?" As I remember it, there was an edge to my voice, not accusatory but angry. Under the circumstances a not unusual feeling, according to the psychiatrist I later saw.

"Lana. It was an accident. You must believe me. Do you believe me?"

"Yes. But what happened?"

"I don't know. Chris and I were talking and she went off to bed. She must have fallen overboard or something like that."

"Didn't you hear her hit the water?"

"I didn't hear a thing."

"Had you all been drinking?"

"Yes, yes, of course. It was after a big dinner on shore, and it was late."

There was a pause, and then he continued. "I don't know what happened. If I knew what happened, I'd tell you. Do you believe that?"

"Yes. But how could something like this happen?" My voice was rising, my anger—not at R.J. but at what had happened—was building. I heard my brother-in-law Alexi say, "Calm down, Lana, take it easy."

I started shouting into the phone. "I'm angry. She's my sister and I have a right to be angry. R.J., I'm sorry. If I sound out of control, it's not because of you. It's not directed at you."

I don't remember anything else of the conversation, except that I kept saying, "I'm sorry" to R.J. and he kept saying the same thing to me.

I then went upstairs and washed my hair in the bathroom sink. I usually shampoo in the shower, and hadn't used the sink for this purpose for many years, not since Natalie and I were children and washed our hair in the sink at home. When I was finished, I felt somehow refreshed, curiously ready to confront what had happened and what still had to be done. It was not until many months later that I even remembered washing my hair. I was in shock, but I was—after a fashion—functioning.

Late that afternoon we went to the house Natalie had loved so much. There were quite a few close friends gathered around, but no R.J. I went upstairs and found him sitting on the edge of their bed, weeping. Marion Donen Wagner was with him, consoling him and talking to him. I hugged him and held him for a time, but there was no reaching through his grief, no way in. Not then. It was too personal, too private.

Downstairs I discovered that Evan had gone to sleep on the living-room sofa. She was out like a light. I went into the bar, sat in the same chair I always sat in when Natalie and I were talking, and wept. Then I picked up the phone and began calling all of our many relatives to tell them when the funeral would be.

Alan, who had just begun performances of *A View from the Bridge* at the Long Wharf Theater in New Haven, Connecticut, flew home. I had managed somehow to keep myself together, but as soon as we were alone together I fell into thousands of emotionally destroyed fragments. I was, Alan said, beginning to express my grief.

We were all instructed to arrive early for the funeral because large crowds were expected, and R.J. wanted everything to run on schedule so that the children wouldn't have to wait any longer than necessary. We were alone in the funeral parlor when Courtney asked to have the coffin opened for one last look at her mother. R.J. gave his permission, and he and Courtney went and stood for a moment at the casket. The rest of us didn't. I didn't want to see her that way, to remember her dead. I wanted to remember her in other ways. The last time I had seen her alive had been Thanksgiving Day.

The funeral was held in the small chapel and cemetery in Westwood, just off Wilshire Boulevard, the same cemetery where Marilyn Monroe is buried. It was a funeral befitting a woman who was much loved in her profession and who had been a great star. I kept a tight grip on Mom's arm—she was now on a new medication and somewhat tranquilized—and Alan kept a tight grip on mine. Evan had chosen to stay close to her cousins, and so I kept glancing at her, making sure she was all right. The crowd was very large. Everyone from Elizabeth Taylor to crews who had worked on Natalie's last film came. It was big, it was loving, and because of all that, it was also comforting. I have the little pamphlet that was printed for the occasion, but I have absolutely no memory of what was said in the course of the funeral itself. I was somewhere else, in another time, remembering.

I had wanted it to be a cold, overcast day, with rain. That, it seemed to me, was how funerals were to be. Instead, it was one of those clear, bright, mercilessly cheerful California early-winter days, and I noticed that nearly everybody was wearing colored glasses— the sunlight an excuse, the tears the reason.

I could see the tears in R.J.'s eyes, and the whiteness of his hands as he held on to his daughters. He had wept openly at the house, and had made no attempt to hide his emotions. I thought it uncharacteristic of him and admired him for it.

We all went back to the house afterward. It seemed to me that everybody was there, everybody I'd ever seen at Natalie's parties, on her sets, and at the big occasions in her life. There was endless food, prepared by Willie Mae. The house, which was big, had never been so full of people. I don't ever recall feeling crowded in it, but this time I did. At one point I eased my way to the bathroom, only to find the door locked. I waited outside for what seemed an unusually long time, and finally Chris Walken emerged,

looking a bit odd. He said nothing, hardly even nodded, and before long he left.

Finally it was over. The relatives all left, Alan went
back to New Haven, and life resumed. Mom immediately asked to come and live with us for a while, and I
burst into tears when she asked because I immediately remembered my promise to Natalie. I think,
under the circumstances, Natalie would have understood. Mom, Evan, and I stayed close together for
the next weeks, and I spoke daily with Alan. We heard
nothing from R.J.

The producer I was working for had been after me
to pitch a story to Warren, so a few days after the
funeral I did. I didn't want to go, but it was my job—
and I felt certain that Warren would turn the project
down. He did, but not before listening to me politely.

"They sent you here because you know me. They
know I'd never listen to anybody else under these
circumstances."

"I know, Warren, but that's how this business
works, isn't it? I know a lot of people. So do you."

Natalie was not mentioned until I was about to
leave, and then I couldn't help it. I wanted him to say
something about her, to say how he would remember
her. I wanted to know that it had been all right between them, between us all, at the end.

"Do you miss Natalie?" I asked Warren.

"No, not really. She's gone and I'm sorry, but
that's it. The truth is that I talked to you and know
you better."

He reached out and pulled me to him. Warren

simply could not let the opportunity get by. This time I could, though.

"Good-bye, Warren," I said as I ran out the door and jumped into my car. He could see my anger, it was right there on my face. He shut the door before I drove off.

Odd things began to happen. I am normally very energetic and capable of doing several things at once. Now, my energy flagged. In the office I would pick up a telephone and be midway into a conversation when I would suddenly realize I didn't know who I was talking to or what had been said. I began to have a great deal of trouble sleeping. I had nightmares, dark dreams in which Natalie would appear and I would awake in tears. Finally I called a psychiatrist.

It took several sessions of pouring out my grief before he sat back and said what I was experiencing was "textbook grief." There was nothing for it but to suffer through it and to go on living. What was particularly difficult for me—and still is, though to a lesser extent—is my lifelong habit of imagining Natalie's reaction to everything I did. Would she approve? Would she be proud? Would she disagree? Would she look up and give me that conspiratorial wink? Never again.

40

I have heard all of the rumors surrounding her death. They began circulating almost immediately. I don't believe any of them. I have also read the coroner's report and have heard what he's had to say subsequently.

My theory, and it is the one most of us who were close to Natalie share, is a simple one. Its simplicity makes it all the more tragic. In the years before she died, the pressures had mounted and Natalie had responded by occasionally drinking too much. She was not an alcoholic by any stretch of the imagination, but it was conceivable that trouble of some sort lay somewhere in the future. She also took sleeping pills—judiciously—and, on occasion, Valium to calm her down. What happened is that Natalie drank too much that night. It didn't take a whole lot, but the coroner's report confirmed that the alcohol in her blood was high, higher than the level at which she'd have been considered a drunk driver.

She got up, put on her heavy down-filled coat, and went out to retie the dinghy the three of them had paddled back from shore a few hours before. It was banging against the side of the boat. She slipped, fell, and went into the water, clinging to the side of the dinghy. At first Thomas Noguchi, the coroner, said she died quickly, and was unconscious almost immediately. We believed she had been spared the agony of confronting her fear of the water. Dr. Noguchi encouraged our belief for more than a year, until he revealed she had struggled, had fought to stay afloat, and was finally pulled under by her down coat. He had withheld the information because at the time he was being severely criticized for his comments about the deaths of William Holden and a number of other celebrities. Dr. Noguchi was subsequently removed from office.

He did, however, create a sensation by saying there was a heated argument going on between R.J. and Chris Walken. Both R.J. and Chris have said it absolutely wasn't so, and I believe them. There was also a report that Natalie and Chris spent the night before she died in a motel on Catalina. Very possibly, but so what? At the bottom of those stories, slipped in almost as a casual aside, is the information they had separate rooms.

Chris is younger than Natalie was. He is very good-looking. He is a New York stage actor. All three things must have appealed mightily to Natalie. She loved the attention she got from him. In the film itself they are trying to revive a troubled marriage, and when it begins to work again their coming together is passionate. It would not have been the first time Natalie fell in love with her leading man; the great tragedy was that it would be the last time.

Her career was not going well, at least not as well as she wanted it to. Some people find consolation in work, Natalie found hers in success, success as it is defined in Hollywood. That means hit films, awards, and stardom. At the end she still had stardom, but that was not enough for Natalie. She made cracks about one day being as fat as Elizabeth Taylor and just as addicted to attention and adulation as Elizabeth was.

"God, I hope I have enough sense not to be that pathetic," she told me.

"I don't think you have anything to worry about."

"On one level I know that, know it absolutely. Another part of me, however, remains to be convinced."

Her marriage was considered to be one of the best in Hollywood, and there is no question that she was a devoted, loving—even adoring—mother and step-mother. She and R.J. had begun with love and built from there. They had overcome each other's problems and had reached an accommodation with time, and the changes time brings. As with anybody else who has settled into making a long marriage work— and they were far more determined than most people to make it work—there was bound to be occasional boredom and restlessness.

Even an occasional infidelity. There are two kinds of infidelity in this world: imaginary and real. Show me a husband or a wife who doesn't occasionally imagine a love affair and I'll show you a liar. Or a fool. I don't know if Natalie's with Chris was imaginary or real, though my strong suspicion is that it was all in her mind and that perhaps she was only wishing it to be so. Whatever. She would never have allowed such a thing to threaten either her marriage or her children.

I thought about it a great deal in the weeks and months after her funeral, and my final thought was always this: I hoped—I prayed—that her imagination was playing out a long and happy scene for her as she died, and that her last thoughts gave her pleasure.

The speculation was still going on a full year after her death. Chris has maintained complete silence. So has everybody else who was involved. In my case, the silence from R.J. has been almost total. At first I was not distressed by the lack of communication from him. I offered myself all sorts of rationalizations: I was a painful reminder, I looked too much like Natalie, and on and on. I even acknowledged what I had known for quite a long time: R.J. had never liked me a whole lot. He accepted me because I was his wife's sister and that was pretty much it. I had been trouble for him when I was a teenager, and I had caused disruptions in his life since. I had hoped the bad feelings had long since vanished, but they have not. I am sorry they exist.

Mom sees him from time to time, usually when she calls and wants to visit the studio to watch the filming of *Hart to Hart* or when she's at the house visiting her granddaughters. She is very careful what she says about him to me, and she is afraid he will get angry with her and not allow her to see Natalie's daughters.

I've told myself time will heal everything. I may even be right, but so much time has gone by that I very much doubt it.

Natalie's will was complicated, in part because she had invested wisely and was enormously wealthy at the time of her death. She owned office buildings, shopping centers, the works. I had known this but hadn't given it a great deal of thought over the years. It was, Natalie had said, her money working for her. She had done everything on the advice of her business manager and lawyers. Almost everything was left to R.J. and the girls, which is as it should be. The most poignant request in the will was that the three children be permitted to grow up together as one family, with R.J. the head of that family. It was a plea to Richard Gregson and Marion Wagner to allow their children to grow up in another household, in Richard's case with another man as Natasha's father. Natalie's request was granted.

Natalie's will also stipulated that should R.J. die, my mom was to raise the kids. Natalie had crossed that out and initialed "N.W." in the margin in ink. Next came Olga as guardian, and if Olga died, Mart Crowley and Howard Jeffries would decide how the kids should be raised. I was hurt that I appeared nowhere in this succession of contingencies.

Mom was allowed to live in the condominium in West Los Angeles and the will assured her of some seven thousand dollars a year. It wasn't a lot, but with her Social Security and the money Dad left, she's making it.

Natalie's bequest to me was a surprise. She left me all of her clothing and all of her furs. Even the lavish Blackglama she had just been given for posing for one of those "What Becomes a Legend Most?" ads. The ads were published one month before her death. I had known Natalie was a clothes horse, but I had no idea of the extent of it. The will also said that if I died before Natalie—or within thirty days of her death— the clothes and furs were to be sold and the proceeds were to be put in the children's trust fund.

It was a wonderful, generous thing for her to do. She knew I had money problems, that Evan was in a private school, and that I was doing it all on my own. It wasn't until after she was gone that her friend Donfeld, the designer—he designed her clothes for *Brainstorm*—wrote me to say the last time he had seen Natalie she had been boasting to him about how well I was doing both in production and as a single mother. His letter filled me with happiness, because it gave me something I had always wanted from Natalie and loved whenever I got it: her approval.

I waited several months, and on a weekend when I had free use of a friend's van, I called to ask if it would be okay to come and pick up the clothes and the furs. Willie Mae answered and said she'd get back to me. She called back within minutes to say yes.

The sheer amount of clothing Natalie owned was beyond even what I had imagined. I knew she had a huge closet—I'd seen it dozens of times. What I didn't know was that other closets in the house were filled with her things. Some clothing, when she no longer wanted it or didn't like it, she sold to several resale shops, but most she kept. I was shaking as I walked into her bedroom, and I was standing there crying when R.J. walked into the room.

He was cordial but cool. We exchanged greetings and then he asked me if it would be okay if he kept the furs and the ski clothes for the girls.

"Of course. Anything you want." Anything to keep the peace.

"I'll pay for them."

"Anything you say, R.J."

"Do you need some help?"

"No, no thanks." I'd brought a couple of friends to help load the clothing but by now I was having second thoughts. "I think I'd leave everything for one little memento," I said to him. Tears were dripping off my cheeks and landing on my chest.

He left the room and returned a few minutes later with a big oil portrait of Natalie, one that had been hanging in the hallway of the house.

"Here. Take this. It's the girls' and they want you and Evan to have it."

I dissolved, and R.J. waved away my thanks with a pat on the back. "Now, take the clothes. They're yours."

It took six trips in the van to gather Natalie's clothes. They filled every available space in my large two-bedroom-and-den apartment. The sheer volume overwhelmed us. My daughter could not sleep in her own bed, as the room was filled with eleven racks (rented) of clothing.

I took down all of the pictures on the big oak wall above my fireplace and hung Natalie's portrait there. It now dominates the mantel of the apartment where I'm currently living, and it is a gift I treasure, a memento I will keep with me for the rest of my life. I also have the photograph that was taken of Natalie as Anastasia to promote the play. It is a remarkable photo which captures her dark beauty, her intensity, and her determination. The painting, the photograph—that is how I choose to remember her.

I began sorting through the clothes. We were the same size; nearly all of them fit me. I began choosing those I wanted to keep, and the rest I decided to sell —just as Natalie had done with the things she didn't want. Keeping everything was impossible unless I rented storage space or found myself an apartment at least twice again as large. There was no way I'd ever wear it all, nor could anyone! Several weeks later, four van loads of clothing went one by one to the four resale shops I knew Natalie used. I came home with almost fifteen thousand dollars. I was certain that was what Natalie had intended, because her will stipulated that the clothing should be sold.

R.J.'s attorneys called a short while later and said they had a check for the furs. But before they'd give it to me I had to go to their offices and sign release forms. Death is a very personal thing, but its consequences on the survivors are often cold, distasteful, and extremely impersonal. I had given my word and I disliked the idea of being made to sign a release, a release which said in fact my claims against Natalie's estate had been satisfied. My objection had nothing to do with R.J. or the release. I don't imagine he even knew of the requirement. To make matters worse, the day of my appointment, I had the flu. I arrived feverish, irritable, and could barely conceal the fact that I also felt insulted. I signed everything without reading one bit of it. I even suppressed a whoop of surprise when I saw the check: it was for twenty thousand dollars.

I saved my whoop until I got home. Alan politely asked if it was enough, considering I had said there had been six or eight furs in the closet, everything from mink to sable. He was thinking of my best interests and suggested I call R.J. and ask about it. He also understood perfectly when I said I couldn't.

Weeks later word came back to me that R.J. was furious that I'd gone out and sold Natalie's clothing. I asked Mom if he'd said anything to her, and she was the picture of innocence. I called him immediately and when he had not returned my call within a day, I called again. There was no answer. And so I wrote to him. There was no response.

My only source of news about R.J. and my nieces was Mom. She, who refused to intervene with Natalie for fear of banishment, was now terrified of having her visits to her granddaughters cut off. She chose to pretend nothing was the matter. Her visits with her grandchildren were infrequent, sometimes months apart, and it wasn't until nearly a year after Natalie was dead that she took Evan with her to see her cousins.

On R.J.'s first birthday after Natalie's death I was afraid he'd be alone. Alan and I shopped for gifts and I bought him a pair of antique wire glove stretchers, because R.J. loves antique curiosities, and Alan got him a bottle of champagne. I rang the house and Katie answered. I asked her when R.J. was coming home from work so we could bring our gifts. She hesitantly informed me she had planned a party for R.J.

"Oh," I stammered.

"It's a lot of people I didn't think you'd know or be comfortable with."

"Such as?" I said.

"Mart Crowley."

"But, Katie, I've known Mart since I was fifteen. We'll be there at seven-thirty. We won't stay long."

At the party R.J. was distant. Alan and I sat at the bar and had a couple of drinks. We made excuses and left as people continued to arrive and the party went on.

Before this, I had not been able to accept that R.J. was uptight with me. Now I knew. I later sent a note. In it I begged him to explain to me what made him angry and urged him to discuss it with me so that I could at least defend myself. There was no response.

I did not see R.J. or my nieces again until we all returned to the cemetery on the anniversary of Natalie's death, a Russian Orthodox tradition we all knew Natalie liked. I considered writing R.J. and offering

not to come if it would upset him, but I wanted—
needed—to be there and so I didn't write. The psychiatrist I had seen for a brief time after Natalie's
death had said I was beginning to transfer my need
for approval from Natalie to R.J., and that, he
stressed, was a serious mistake. For the first time
after months of feeling like an outcast, a social crimi-
nal of some sort, of wondering why there was no
response to my calls or letters, I said to hell with R.J.
and went.

Evan was excited about seeing her cousins and
took three of her treasured ceramics, a collection of
animals and toys, and wrapped them, one each for
Katie, Natasha, and Courtney. I was touched by her
generosity and watched as she gave them their
presents. Katie, who was old enough to understand
the significance of the gifts, made sure her sisters
reacted accordingly. I watched the exchange from
the side of the small group gathered for the occasion.
R.J. looked up when he saw me, then walked over,
kissed me on the cheek, and said hello. That was all.
After the brief ceremony, Mom came up and said she
wouldn't need a ride home—she was going to R.J.'s
house with the others. No invitation was issued to
either Evan or me. I went home and wept, wept as
much as I had the day of Natalie's death.

It has taken me well over a year to go from being
ashamed of whatever it is I've done to being hurt and
angry. Then one day I actually got furious and made
sure everybody knew it.

R.J. had moved out of the house on Canon Drive

and into another house in Pacific Palisades, one where the girls could keep horses. I can understand his wanting to move, and I said so to everyone who asked. Then one day Mom took Evan to the new house and came back to my apartment with Natasha. Natasha, so that she could remember to call and say where she was, had written her new phone number down on a piece of paper. I scooped up Natasha, gave her a big kiss, then went about my business while they played and Mom read. After a while, Mom announced they were all going to R.J.'s for an early dinner.

"Fine, Mom. Have a good time, girls!" I was trying to act casual and I expect it looked just like that: trying.

A few months before, I had come home from the office and discovered Mom's glasses, her blood-pressure pills, and her apartment keys on the table. No Mom, no Evan. I began worrying because I knew Mom never went anywhere without her glasses, keys, and pills. Six hours later I began to panic. There was nothing to do but wait. Six hours later they came home. I made the rule that very night: Mom was not to take Evan out without first leaving the phone number where they were going and an approximate time they'd be home.

Mom had observed the rule well, and that night, after Natasha and Evan had gone out the door and were waiting in the car for Mom, I walked by the phone and noticed Natasha's piece of paper with her number written on it. I thought no more of it until

several hours later, when it began to get late—too
late for a school night. I went to call them, and the
phone number was gone.

The confrontation that followed when they got
home was as hard for Mom as it was for me. I knew
neither Evan nor Natasha had picked up the piece of
paper. They had already gone when I'd last seen it.
The implication was clear. I was not to be allowed to
have the telephone number at R.J.'s new house. I
spared her having to tell me whether it had been
done at R.J.'s instruction or on her own. She was
either evasive or distraught. I restated the rule and
said there was never to be an exception.

"Don't tell R.J.," Mom said as she wrote it down.

"Don't worry."

In the months and now years since Natalie's death
I have spoken to R.J. three times. Once when I picked
up Natalie's clothing and once at the graveside on
the first anniversary of her death. The third time was
on the telephone—and that because I think he was
embarrassed into it. A voice, unmistakably R.J.'s,
called and asked to speak to Mom. I put her on. They
chatted several minutes—something to do with logistics involving a visit to the set of *Hart to Hart* by Mom,
Evan, and Courtney—and then Mom, casual as you
please, handed the phone to me.

"He wants to speak to you."

He asked how I was, what I was doing. I told him I
was fine, that I was working for a producer who was
well known for overreacting to the pressures of producing and that as soon as I was certain of my asso-

ciate-producer credit on the movie-of-the-week we were making I was quitting. I told him I loved producing. I said that producing came first now, acting second, and that I was considering an offer to join the cast on *Capitol*, a soap which held out the possibility of an income and enough days off to pursue producing. I was so pleased he asked, I just blurted it all out. Finally I got around to asking him how he was. Fine, he said, and then he made a couple of jokes about my employer. And that was it.

Why didn't I confront him? Why didn't I ask what was the matter? It's just not in my nature to do so. I had tried, and had been rebuffed, and that is too painful. I have been convicted of a crime. I don't know what the crime is, but that doesn't seem to matter to anybody but me. I still see our mutual friends, and they profess to know nothing about it. I stopped asking long ago.

I know only this. Natalie is gone. The person I loved more than anybody else, with the sole exception of my own daughter, is dead. I cry for her often. I expect I always will.

41

After a year of litigation over whether to release it, *Brainstorm* finally opened on September 30, 1983. I read the interviews and the reviews, and depending on who you were reading, it was either Natalie's best performance (this from an interview with Douglas Trumbull, the director) or one of her less consequential (which seemed to be the consensus of the critics, though it was always carefully and politely stated). I decided not to see the film, but finally the chance to look at her as she was at the very end of her life was just too much. Alan, Evan, and I went to a big theater in Hollywood, where all of the special effects and Natalie's beauty could be seen in seventy-millimeter.

I know exactly what Natalie would have said about it. She would have summoned up all of her feisty spirit, shrugged her shoulders, and said, "Well, I guessed wrong again!" She would have been dismayed over her portrayal, certainly those parts in which she was playing the businesswoman, the designer of the headset which allowed those wearing it to experience the sensations of others. Natalie was

318

smart, particularly about her own work. She would
have seen that she was stiff and uncomfortable in
those scenes. She was right when she had said the
real stars of *Brainstorm* were the special effects. I think
she would have tried hard to be understanding when
she saw that both Chris Walken and Louise Fletcher
had far more substantial roles than she had. That
certainly had not been her understanding when she
had begun work on the film.

She would have been pleased with her scenes with
Chris. They show Natalie at her best, one-on-one,
caring, thoughtful, romantic, and very, very sexy.
She would have been pleased that her best scene in
the picture wasn't even in the script. It was her idea.

In the film, Natalie and Chris are estranged, but
through the device that transfers the emotions and
memories of one person to another, they are able to
relive their time together and, in the process, end
their separation and become lovers once again. They
are sitting on their bed, locked in an embrace, two
beautiful bodies barely glimpsed beneath the sheet
that covers them. Natalie begins to sing a tone poem
from Mel Brooks and Carl Reiner's comedy album
The 2001-Year-Old-Man. It is a nonsensical little poem
having to do with the hope that everybody in the
world should feel good and stop being so nervous.
As Brooks did it, it was hilarious. But when Natalie
and I first heard the album, the poem had a special
meaning to us. We were trying hard to sort our way
through the complexities of the world, and had taken
time out to spend an evening sitting on the floor

listening to records. We adored it. In its wacky philo-
sophical way, it spoke to us, meant something to us.

When she repeated it in *Brainstorm,* I was suddenly
back on that floor, my legs crossed, my ear tuned to
Natalie's voice. Up until that moment it had struck
me that this was a film about death, about dying and
deceit. Then, for a moment, *Brainstorm*'s plot became, for me, something quite literal, transporting
me back to that evening with Natalie and giving me a
memory to cherish. And it helped me to realize that,
in my way, I had to make peace with my memories.